OFFICE TO OFFICE

Practical Business Communication

K Methold and J Tadman

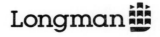

Longman

Contents

PART ONE

UNIT 1

Inquiries (1)

Tom Standish is the sales manager of World Wide Travel Ltd., a large travel agency. Sue Downing is his secretary. The morning post has arrived. Sue hasn't taken it in to Tom yet. She is still opening it. Tom is always interested in his mail. He walks out of his office and goes to Sue's desk.

TOM: Is there anything interesting in the post, Sue?

SUE: Yes. We've had a reply from Charter Airways. They've sent us their new fare schedule.

TOM: Ah, good. I'm interested in that airline. They've got some good ideas. I think we can use them.

SUE: And there are some replies to our advertisement in 'Travel Magazine'. And to the brochures and circulars.

TOM: Excellent. I'd like to look at them. Will you bring them into my office, please? Then I'd like you to answer them as soon as possible. We must reply to inquiries quickly.

SUE: Yes, of course. I'll deal with them today.

1

Talking about the dialogue

A

True or false? Correct the false statements.
1 Tom and Sue are talking about the morning's post.
F 2 Charter Airways has replied to World Wide Travel Ltd.'s advertisement.
3 World Wide Travel Ltd. (W.W.T.) has had an advertisement in 'Travel Magazine'.
4 Tom isn't interested in the replies to the advertisement.
5 Sue hasn't answered any of the letters yet.
6 Tom will answer the letters as soon as possible.

B

Answer these questions in complete sentences.
1 What has Charter Airways sent to W.W.T.?
2 Why is Tom interested in Charter Airways?
3 What are the other letters about?
4 Why hasn't Sue answered the letters yet?
5 What does Tom want Sue to do?

Practice exercises

A

Mary Jones is the clerk in W.W.T.'s sales department. She often helps Sue open the letters and check advertisements in newspapers and magazines. Sue and Mary are talking about the new fare schedule in the post from Charter Airways:

SUE: Is there anything **interesting** in the post, Mary?

MARY: Yes. There's a new fare schedule from Charter Airways.

SUE: Good. Tom will be **interested** in that.

Working in pairs, talk about the following in the same way.
1 'Holiday Magazine'—an advertisement for Travel Planners Ltd.
2 that circular—details of the new rail fares
3 the mail—some inquiries about tours
4 that brochure—a list of low-priced hotels
5 that advertisement—details of charter flights to Hong Kong
6 those letters—replies to circulars

B

Mary's desk is in the main office of W.W.T. She has to deal with most of the customers. Just now she is talking to Mr Smith. He wants to fly to Paris on Thursday:

MARY: Good morning, sir. Can I help you?

SMITH: Er, yes. **I'd like to** fly to Paris.

MARY: Yes, of course. When **would you like to** go?

SMITH: **I'd like to** go on Thursday.

Working in pairs, talk about the following in the same way.
1　Mrs Wilson wants to buy a ticket for Rome on Sunday 11th May.
2　Miss Thomas wants to go on an Historic Britain tour in early June.
3　Mr Mori wants to return to Tokyo tomorrow.
4　Mrs Evans wants to have a holiday in Tasmania in the autumn.
5　Mr Strong wants to spend a week in Hamburg from 10th May.
6　Mr Obuko wants to fly to Mombasa as soon as possible.
7　Mr Edwards wants to sail to New York on the next ship.
8　Miss Hunt wants to visit a friend in Majorca in June.

C

Practise using would like to *with* Where *and* How. *Ask and answer questions using these tables.*

Where		stay?
	would you like to	
How		go/travel?

	stay at	the Ritz Hotel. any cheap hotel. any medium-priced hotel. the best hotel. the Y.M.C.A./Y.W.C.A.
I'd like to		
	go by	air/air France/BMA./etc. sea/ship/the Q.E.2. rail/train. road/coach/bus/car.

D

Using the patterns in B and C, make up conversations like this:

MARY:　Can I help you?

CUSTOMER:　Yes. **I'd like to** go to Paris.

MARY:　Yes, sir/madam. **When would you like to** go?

CUSTOMER:　Next Thursday.

MARY:　**How would you like to** go, sir/madam?

CUSTOMER:　By air. And **I'd like to** stay at the Ritz Hotel.

E

Tom is polite to his staff. He does not give them orders. He did not say to Sue:
　"Bring them [the letters] into my office."
He asked her:
　"**Will you** bring them into my office, **please?**"

3

How would Tom ask members of his staff to do the following?
1 Bring his letters into his office.
2 Send out the circulars to the new customers.
3 Reply to the inquiries.
4 Get a fare schedule from British Airways.
5 Put the brochures into envelopes.
6 Deal with the mail.
7 Help Mary in the main office.
8 Open the letters for Sue.

The letters

A

```
                                           2-2 Kanda Jimbocho,
                                           Chiyoda-ku,
                                           Tokyo 101,
                                           Japan

            The Sales Manager,             4th February 198-
            World Wide Travel Ltd.,
            14 Old Oxford Street,
            London W1 4X
            England

            Dear Sir,
                     I have seen your advertisement in this week's 'Travel
            Magazine', and am interested in your Historic Britain tours.

                     Please send me your illustrated brochure and full details
            of prices.

                              Yours faithfully,

                              T. Suzuki

                              T. Suzuki
```

Compare the forms of address in the three letters:
A *Dear Sir* — to the Sales Manager
B *Dear Sirs* — to the company as a whole, UK style
C *Gentlemen* — American style (= Dear Sirs)

Compare also the endings:
A/B Yours faithfully—formal, UK
C   Sincerely yours—formal, USA

Answer these questions in complete sentences.
1 What is Mr Suzuki replying to?
2 What is he interested in?
3 What does he want W.W.T. to send him?

B

```
                                          9 Avenue du Bijou,
                                          01201 Ferney-Voltaire,
                                          Paris,
                                          France

     World Wide Travel Ltd.,              1st February 198-
     14 Old Oxford Street,
     London W1 4X
     England

     Dear Sirs,

            With reference to your advertisement in this month's issue
     of 'Visit Britain', I am interested in your Seven Day Coach and Rail
     tours.  I should like to receive full details of these tours at your
     earliest convenience.

                    Yours faithfully,

                    Simone Chardin

                    Simone Chardin (Miss)
```

Answer these questions in complete sentences.
1 What is Miss Chardin replying to?
2 What is she interested in?
3 What would she like to receive?

C

```
                                          Lions Club of Atlanta,
                                          1515 Main Street,
                                          Georgia 876352,
                                          U.S.A.

     World Wide Travel Ltd,               February 1st, 198-
     14 Old Oxford Street,
     London W1 4X
     England

     Gentlemen:

            I have received your circular 'Holidays in Britain'.
     Would you please send me full details of group tour rates as
     soon as possible.

                    Sincerely yours,

                    Edward J. Blavetsky

                    Edward J. Blavetsky
                    Secretary, Travel Committee
```

Answer these questions in complete sentences.
1 What has Mr Blavetsky received?
2 What does he want to receive?

Practice exercises

A

Miss Chardin saw a W.W.T. advertisement. She began her letter:
> "**With reference to** your advertisement in this month's issue of 'Visit Britain', **I am interested in** your Seven Day Coach and Rail tours."

In the same way, write the first sentence of your letters in response to the following:
1 You have seen a Parker advertisement in 'The Times'. You are interested in their range of pens.
2 You have seen a Philips advertisement in 'Time' magazine. You are interested in their special colour TV offer.
3 You have seen a Heinz advertisement on television. You are interested in their cookery courses.

Now begin 1—3 in the same way as Mr Suzuki:
> "**I have seen** your advertisement in ... **and am interested in ...**"

B

Mr Suzuki saw a W.W.T. advertisement in 'Travel Magazine'. He wanted W.W.T.'s illustrated brochure. He also wanted details of prices. He wrote:
> "**Please send** me your illustrated brochure **and** details of prices."

In the same way, write the last sentence of your letters in response to the following:
1 You have received a circular from Bargain Stores. You want their catalogue. You also want their price list.
2 You have received a brochure from Asian Airways. You want their schedule. You also want details of cheap fares.
3 You have seen an advertisement for International Correspondence Schools. You want a copy of their prospectus. You also want details of charges.

C

Miss Chardin wants full details of the Seven Day Rail and Coach tours. She wrote:
> "**I should like to** receive full details of these tours at your earliest convenience."

In the same way, write letters asking for the following:
1 an illustrated brochure/as soon as possible
2 full details of prices/at your earliest convenience
3 latest catalogue/by return of post
4 price list/by airmail
5 full details/by first class mail

Now ask for the same things in the same way as Mr Blavetsky:
> "**Would you please** send me ..."

D

*Study the advertisements and write letters of inquiry to each adver-
tiser. Use as many of the sentence patterns and expressions that you
have studied in this unit as you can, so that each of your letters is
different in some way from the others.*

Four wonderful ways to get away between April and August

Get some sun, enjoy life on one of the world's great cruise liners,
and get away to a new and relaxing world. Enjoy the sun,
the sea air, interesting places, good food, superb entertainment
on a holiday that's different from any other.

To Greece & Corfu
May 31–June 14, Cruise 006 visiting **Palma** (Majorca), **Loutraki** (for Corinth and Athens), **Corfu**, **Messina** (Sicily) and **Gibraltar**. 14 nights from £472.
CURRENT BROCHURE PRICES GUARANTEED ON THIS CRUISE

To Norway & The Fjords
June 14–29, Cruise 008 visiting **Bergen, Sogne Fjord, Narvik, Spitzbergen** and **Isfjord, Trondheim, Oslo, Cuxhaven** (for Hamburg). 15 nights for £513.
CURRENT BROCHURE PRICES GUARANTEED ON THIS CRUISE

To Spain, Provence & Florence
June 22–July 5, Cruise 009 visiting **Cadiz, Marseilles** (for Avignon and Aix), **Leghorn** (for Florence and Pisa), **Ibiza, Lisbon**. 13 nights from £440.

To Spain, North Africa and the Islands
July 19–August 1, Cruise 013 visiting **Cadiz, Casablanca** (for Marrakesh), **Lanzarote** (Canaries), **Madeira, Ponta Delgada** (Azores). 13 nights from £446.

NO SURCHARGES IF YOU PAY FULL FARE WITHIN 12 DAYS OF INVOICE

Write for free brochure to:
Sundeck Cruises, P.O. Box 123, Bristol BS20 6ST

Name _____
Address _____

7

UNIT 2

Replies to inquiries (1)

Mary is speaking on the telephone to Mr Wilson. He is an American on holiday in Britain.

MARY: (*on the phone*) World Wide Travel. Good morning. Can I help you?

WILSON: (*on the phone*) Oh, good morning. Er, yes, I've just seen your advertisement in 'Travel Magazine'. I'd like some information about your Historic Britain tours. Can you send it to me?

MARY: Of course, sir. I'll be pleased to send it to you. May I have your name and address?

WILSON: Wilson. Harry J. Wilson. Room 402. Thameside Hotel.

MARY: Thank you, Mr Wilson. I'll post a brochure to you today.

WILSON: Many thanks.

MARY: And please don't hesitate to contact us if you need any more information.

WILSON: Right. I won't.

MARY: I'll look forward to making a reservation for you, Mr Wilson. Thank you for calling. Goodbye.

WILSON: Goodbye.

Talking about the dialogue

A

True or false? Correct the false statements.
1 Mr Wilson came to W.W.T.'s office.
2 He was interested in the Historic Britain tours.
3 Mary gave him a lot of information over the phone.
4 Mary made a reservation for him.
5 If Mr Wilson wants more information he can phone W.W.T. again.
6 He will receive a brochure from W.W.T.

B

Answer these questions in complete sentences.
1 Why did Mr Wilson telephone W.W.T.?
2 What will Mary send him?
3 Where is he staying?
4 Why, do you suppose, is he interested in the Historic Britain tours?
5 What does Mary hope she can do for him?

Practice exercises

A

Mr Wilson wants some information about the Historic Britain tours. Mary can send it to him. He said:
    "I'd like some information about the Historic Britain tours. **Can you send it to me?**"
She said:
    "Of course, sir. I'll be **pleased to** send it to you."

In pairs, make conversations about the following in the same way.

Use I'll be {pleased / glad / delighted} to ...

1 Mr Muller is interested in Charter Airways' fare schedule. You can tell him about it.
2 Mr Provenzano would like to fly to Rome tomorrow. You can make a reservation for him.
3 Mrs Wong wants to stay in a good hotel in Paris. You can recommend one.
4 Miss Palmer wants an interesting holiday. You can make some suggestions.
5 Mr Tanaka wants to fly to Tokyo as soon as possible. You can help him.
6 Mr Obuko wants to know if there is a plane to Kampala tomorrow. You can find out for him.
7 Mr Robinson is planning his holiday. You can let him have some brochures.

B

Mr Wilson *called* W.W.T. on the telephone. At the end of the conversation Mary said:

"**Thank you for** calling."

How did she thank these people?
1 Mr Smith, who *let her know* he could not fly to Paris on Wednesday.
2 Mr Johnson, who *came* into the office for some brochures.
3 Sue, who *gave her some advice.*
4 Mary's friend, who *phoned* her.
5 Charter Airways, who *sent their new schedule.*
6 Freddie, the office boy, who *helped her with the post.*

C

Mary hopes she will be able to make a reservation for Mr Wilson. She said:

"I'll **look forward to** making a reservation for you, Mr Wilson."

What would these people say?
1 Mr Wilson, who hopes he will receive a brochure.
2 Mary, who hopes she will hear from Mr Wilson again soon.
3 Sue, who hopes she will get some advice from Mr Standish.
4 Mary, who hopes she will see her friend next week.
5 Mr Standish, who hopes he will assist Mr Johnson.
6 Miss Palmer, who hopes she will get her ticket soon.

D

Work in pairs. Offer further services and reply using the tables.

Please	(don't hesitate to)	phone call in let us know tell us contact us inform us

if you	want need require 'd like	any further information, an illustrated brochure, any advice, a reservation, more details, any help,	Mr Wilson. Miss Palmer. Mrs Smith. etc.

I certainly will.
Yes, I will. Thank you.
No, I won't. Thank you very much.
Right, I won't.

Example (a): x: **Please don't hesitate to let us know** if you need a reservation, Mrs Smith.

               Y: No, I won't. Thank you very much.

Example (b): x: **Please let us know** if you need a reservation, Mrs Smith.

               Y: Yes, I will. Thank you.

E

Now repeat Exercise D, beginning with If . . .

Example: If you require any more details, please (don't hesitate to) let us know.

The letters

A

World Wide Travel Ltd. 14 Old Oxford Street, London W14X, England

Tel: 0473281   Telegrams: WORTRAV London   Telex: WT 9876

Mr T. Suzuki,   our ref: TS/SD
2-2 Kanda Jimbocho,
Chiyoda-ku,
Tokyo 101,
Japan   12th February 198-

Dear Mr Suzuki,

Thank you for your letter of 4th February, inquiring about our Historic Britain tours. We have pleasure in sending you our illustrated brochure and price list.

We hope you will find it of interest, and look forward to making your travel arrangements.

Yours sincerely,

T. Standish

T. Standish
Sales Manager

Enc. 1

Answer these questions in complete sentences.
1 What did **Mr Suzuki** inquire about?
2 What did W.W.T. send him?
3 What are W.W.T. looking forward to?

B

World Wide Travel Ltd., 14 Old Oxford Street, London W14X, England

Tel: 0473281   Telegrams: WORTRAV London   Telex: WT 9876

Miss Simone Chardin,   our ref: TS/SD
9 Avenue du Bijou,
01201 Ferney-Voltaire,
Paris,
France   12th February 198-

Dear Miss Chardin,

In reply to your inquiry of 1st February, we have pleasure in
enclosing full details of our Seven Day Coach and Rail tours.
If you require any additional information, please do not hesitate
to contact us.

We look forward to making reservations for you on the tour of
your choice.

Yours sincerely,

S. Downing

Sales Department

Enc. 1

Answer these questions in complete sentences.
1   What is this letter a reply to?
2   What is enclosed with this letter?
3   What does it invite Miss Chardin to do?

C

World Wide Travel Ltd., 14 Old Oxford Street, London W14X, England

```
Tel:  0473281    Telegrams: WORTRAV London    Telex: WT 9876


Mr Edward J. Blavetsky,                      our ref: TS/SD
Secretary, Travel Committee,
Lions Club of Atlanta,
1315 Main Street,
Georgia 876352,
U.S.A.                                       12th February 198-


Dear Mr Blavetsky,

With reference to your inquiry of 1st February, we are pleased
to send you our 'Holidays in Britain' brochure.  This provides
full details of all our tours in Britain.

In our experience these holidays are especially popular, and
we suggest that you make reservations as early as possible.


Yours sincerely,

T. Standish

T. Standish
Sales Manager


Enc. 1
```

Answer these questions in complete sentences.
1 What does this letter refer to?
2 What details does the brochure give?
3 What does W.W.T. suggest that Mr Blavetsky should do?

Practice exercises

A
On 4th February Mr Suzuki wrote a letter to W.W.T. He inquired about their Historic Britain tours. They replied:
    "**Thank you for your letter** of 4th February, **inquiring** about our Historic Britain tours."

In the same way, write the first sentence of your letters in response to the following:
1 On 9th July, Mr Provenzano wrote a letter to Motor Sport Ltd. He inquired about the Mercedes 350 SL Saloon.
2 On 12th December, Miss Palmer wrote a letter to Office Supplies Ltd. She asked for information on the IBM 90 electric typewriter.

B

On 1st February Miss Chardin wrote to W.W.T. She wanted details of the Seven Day Coach and Rail tours. W.W.T. replied:

"**In reply to** your inquiry of 1st February, we **have pleasure in** enclosing full details of our Seven Day Coach and Rail tours."

In the same way, write the first sentence of your letters in response to the following:
1   On 9th May, Mr Wong wrote to the Parker Pen Company. He wanted details of their range of pens.
2   On 22nd December, Mr Tomkins wrote to Philips Electrical Ltd. He was interested in their special colour TV offer.

C

On 1st February, Mr Blavetsky wrote to W.W.T. He wanted full details of their Holidays in Britain. W.W.T. replied:

"**With reference to** your inquiry of 1st February, we are **pleased to** send you our 'Holidays in Britain' brochure."

In the same way, write the first sentence of your letters in response to the following:
1   On 9th April, Mr Tanaka wrote to Bargain Stores. He asked for their catalogue and price list.
2   On 24th April, Mr Obuko wrote to Asian Airways. He wanted their schedule and details of cheap fares.

D

Rewrite the following statements in a different way.
Example: In reply to your letter of 8th March, we *have pleasure in sending* you our latest catalogue.
              With reference to your letter of 8th March, we **are pleased to send** you our latest catalogue.
1   In reply to your inquiry of 10th June, we have pleasure in enclosing our illustrated brochure.
2   With reference to your letter of 12th August, we are pleased to send you our price list and range of samples.

Now express the same ideas in two statements of your own.
Example: **Thank you for** your letter of 8th March. We **have pleasure in** sending you (**are pleased to send** you) our latest catalogue.

E

Reply to each of the following letters of inquiry. Use the sentence patterns or expressions that you have studied in this unit, so that each of your letters is different from the others.
1   With reference to your advertisement in 'The Times', please send me full details of your publications.
2   I am interested in your range of travel goods, as advertised in 'Holiday Magazine'. Please let me have a copy of your illustrated brochure.
3   With reference to your circular letter, I would like to receive details of your Bargain Record Club.

UNIT 3

Reminder letters

Sue is working at her desk when the phone rings. She answers it.

SUE: Good morning. World Wide Travel. Can I help you?

OPERATOR: Overseas telegrams here. I have a telegram for you. Will you take it down?

SUE: Yes. Go ahead, please.

OPERATOR: (*dictating*) WORTRAV LONDON. Message begins. PLEASE SEND HOLIDAYS BRITAIN BROCHURE REQUESTED MY LETTER 1/2. It's signed BLA-VETSKY. Have you got that?

SUE: Yes. Thank you.

OPERATOR: Do you want a confirmation copy?

SUE: Yes, please.

Sue puts down the phone and goes to the filing cabinet. She takes out the correspondence between W.W.T. and Mr Blavetsky. Then she

15

types out the telegram on a piece of paper and takes it, and the correspondence, into Tom Standish. She hands him the telegram.

SUE: This just came in. Mr Blavetsky wrote on the first and asked us to send him the 'Holidays in Britain' brochure.

TOM: Then why haven't we sent him one yet?

SUE: But we have. (*She hands him a copy of his letter.*)
You replied to his letter on the twelfth. I'm surprised that he hasn't received it yet.

TOM: Mmm. What did I say in reply to his letter?
(*He reads Blavetsky's letter and his own.*) Ah, he was interested in our group rates. Send him a telegram, Sue. And please do it now. Say: Re your letter 1/2 and telegram brochure sent 12/2 stop Another sent today.

Talking about the dialogue

A

True or false? Correct the false statements.
1 Mr Blavetsky telephoned W.W.T.
2 Mr Blavetsky had not received the 'Holidays in Britain' brochure.
3 Sue put a copy of the telegram into the filing cabinet.
4 She gave Tom a copy of his reply to Mr Blavetsky's letter.
5 Tom dictated another letter to Sue.
6 W.W.T. sent Mr Blavetsky another copy of the 'Holidays in Britain' brochure.

B

Answer these questions in complete sentences.
1 Who phoned W.W.T.?
2 What did she dictate?
3 What will she send?
4 Where did Sue find the correspondence between W.W.T. and Mr Blavetsky?
5 What did Tom tell Sue to do?

Practice exercises

A

Tom is talking to Sue about her work:

TOM: **Have you replied** to Mr Muller's letter **yet?**

SUE: Yes, I **have.** I **replied** to it **yesterday.**

Working in pairs, make conversations about the following in the same way.
1 Mrs Jones' inquiry/deal with/this morning
2 Mr Kawasaki's letter/answer/yesterday
3 Miss Palmer's complaint/deal with/on Monday

4   Mrs Wong's list of hotels/type out/this morning
5   Mr Wilson's ticket/make out/on Friday
6   Mr Hess's inquiry/reply to/last week

B

But Sue is not always up-to-date with her work:

TOM: **Have you replied** to Mr Kim's letter **yet**?

SUE: No, **not yet.**

TOM: Then **please reply** to it **immediately.**

Working in pairs, make conversations about the following in the same way.
1   Mrs Johnson's letter/reply to/at once
2   Mr Iwaki's inquiry/deal with/immediately
3   Mr Karumba's complaint/deal with/today
4   Miss Ribiere's ticket/make out/this morning
5   Mrs Gustaffson's telegram/answer/now
6   The new brochures/send out/this week

C

A number of people have complained to W.W.T. recently. Sue dealt with their complaints.

Example:

MR MULLER: I **wrote and asked** for a brochure on the first of February. I **haven't received** it **yet.**

SUE: I'm surprised that you **haven't received** it **yet,** sir. We **sent** it on the fourteenth.

Working in pairs, make conversations about the following in the same way.
1   Miss Palmer/write/ask for/Charter Airways schedule/2nd February ... 12th February
2   Mr Tanaka/come in/pay for/ticket/last week ... the day before yesterday
3   Mrs Wilson/phone/ask for/confirmation of her reservation/last Wednesday ... on the same day
4   Mr Obuko/call in/ask for/list of hotels in Kampala/9th February ... three days ago
5   Miss Ribiere/write/request/details of all tours/last Monday ... the following day

D

Tom Standish wanted to know what the people were complaining about:

Example:

TOM: What did Mr Muller want?

SUE: He **wrote** on the first of February **and asked us to** send him a brochure.

TOM: Oh? Why **hasn't** he **received** it **yet**?

SUE: I don't know. **It was sent** on the fourteenth. I'm surprised he **hasn't already got** it.

TOM: Well, **please send** him another brochure **immediately**.

Working in pairs, make conversations like this, using the information in C above.

The letters

A

```
                                          Flat 4,
                                          18 Old Peak Road,
                                          Hong Kong

   * The Sales Manager,                   18th February 198-
     World Wide Travel Ltd.


     Dear Sir,

            On 3rd February 198- I wrote in response to your advertise-
     ment in 'Travel Magazine' and requested a copy of your brochure and
     price list.  I have not yet received a reply to my letter.  I should
     be grateful if you would send me the brochure without further delay.


                     Yours faithfully,

                     Au Bak Heng

                     Au Bak Heng
```

Answer these questions in complete sentences.
1 What did Mr Au do on 3rd February?
2 What did he ask for?
3 Why has he written to W.W.T. again?

Note: The full address (as in Unit 1, letter A) would always be given here. However, to save space in this book, known addressees and their addresses are not usually repeated.

B

Dear Sirs,   20th February 198-

       I am surprised that I have not received a reply to my inquiry of 1st February, which I wrote in response to your advertisement in 'Visit Britain'. Kindly send me the information which I requested by return of post.

       Yours faithfully,

Simone Chardin

       Simone Chardin (Miss)

Answer these questions in complete sentences.
1 Why is Miss Chardin surprised?
2 What was her inquiry in response to?
3 How soon does she want a reply?

C

                                Av. Pte. Roque Saenz Pena,
                                917 - 70 "R",
                                Buenos Aires,
                                Argentina

World Wide Travel Ltd.   19th February 198-

Gentlemen:

       I have not yet received your brochure and price list for your advertised 'Holiday in Britain', which I requested in my letter of 3rd February.

       I look forward to hearing from you in the immediate future.

       Sincerely yours,

Virgil Contziu
       Virgil Contziu

Answer these questions in complete sentences.
1 What did Mr Contziu request on 3rd February?
2 Why has he written again?
3 What does he want W.W.T. to do?

Practice exercises

A

Mr Contziu wrote to W.W.T. on 3rd February. He requested their brochure and price list. He has not yet received them, so he has written again. He said:

"I have not yet received your brochure and price list . . . , **which I requested** in my letter of 3rd February."

In the same way, write the first sentences of your letters about the following:

1   You wrote to Motor Sport Ltd. on 9th July. You asked for details of the new Mercedes 350 SL Saloon. You have not yet received them.
2   You wrote to Office Supplies Ltd. on 12th December. You requested some information about the IBM 90 electric typewriter. You have not yet received it.
3   You wrote to Modern Photographic Supplies Ltd. on 1st April. You asked for a price list of their range of Kodak cameras. You have not yet received it.

B

On 1st February Miss Chardin wrote a letter of inquiry in answer to W.W.T.'s advertisement in 'Visit Britain'. She is surprised that she has not received a reply. She wrote again:

"I am **surprised that** I have not received a reply to my letter of inquiry of 1st February, **which I wrote in response to** your advertisement in 'Visit Britain'."

In the same way, write the first sentence of your letters expressing surprise at not receiving replies to the following:

1   You received a circular from Bargain Stores and wrote to them on 9th May for further details.
2   You are interested in a special colour TV offer, and wrote to Philips Electrical about it on 22nd December.
3   You saw a Heinz announcement about cookery classes and wrote to them on 9th November.

C

Write four letters, each of two sentences, about the following. Begin two of the letters in the style of A above and the other two in the style of B. End each letter in a different way, using one of the following:

Kindly send me . . . by return of post.
Would you please send me . . . without further delay.
I should be grateful if you would send me . . . in the near future.
I look forward to receiving . . . as soon as possible.

Examples:
10th June—(Asian Airways)—schedule of cheap fares—TV advertisement

(*a*) I have not yet received your schedule of cheap fares, **which I requested** on 10th June. **Kindly send** me the schedule **by return of post.**

(b) I am **surprised that** I have not received a reply to my letter of 10th June, **which I wrote in response to** your TV advertisement. **I look forward to** receiving your schedule of cheap fares **in the near future.**

1   12th October—(International Correspondence School)—prospectus and details of charges—circular
2   25th April—(Better Books Ltd.)—details of publications—advertisement in 'Readers' News'
3   9th August—(Luxury Luggage)—illustrated brochure—special travel goods offer
4   14th July—(Bargain Records)—catalogue—TV advertisement

D

Mr Blavetsky did not write another letter to W.W.T. He sent a telegram instead. He wanted to say:

> Would you please send me your 'Holidays in Britain' brochure, which I requested in my letter of 1st February.

But we pay for a telegram according to the number of words, so he took out all the words that were not necessary for the meaning (shown here in brackets):

> (Would you) PLEASE SEND (me) (your) HOLIDAYS (in) BRITAIN BROCHURE (which) (I) REQUESTED (in) MY LETTER (of) (the) 1/2.

(1/2 means the first day of the second month of the year, i.e. 1st February.) Then he signed only his last name. He also used the telegraphic address: WORTRAV LONDON, a short form of address which can be used only for telegrams.

Rewrite the following in the form of telegrams, replacing longer expressions by single words where possible, for example:

Would you please I should be grateful if you would	PLEASE

in the immediate/near future as soon as possible	IMMEDIATELY SOONEST (= form often used in telegrams but otherwise not equivalent to *as ... as*)

1   Would you please send me by airmail a copy of your prospectus in the immediate future.
2   Please reply to my letter of the 9th of May as soon as possible.
3   Would you please send me by airmail details of your cheap fares.
4   A reply to our letter of the 12th of June has not yet been received.
5   I should be grateful if you would send me your latest prices before the end of May.

UNIT 4

Apologies

Many people have complained to W.W.T. because they have not received replies to their letters of inquiry. Tom Standish is not pleased with the situation. He is discussing it with Sue.

TOM: Look at all these letters, Sue. Not one of them has received a reply.

SUE: Yes, I know. I'm terribly sorry I haven't replied to them yet.

TOM: It's not good enough, Sue. We spend a lot of money advertising for new customers, and then we don't answer their letters.

SUE: But that's the whole trouble. We've had so many inquiries that I haven't been able to cope with them all.

TOM: You've got Mary to help you. Use her!

SUE: But Mary hasn't been able to help much with the letters because she's been so busy on the phone.

22

TOM: What? All day?

SUE: Well, most of it. And anyway, we ran out of brochures. New supplies only came in from the printer this morning.

TOM: Can you send them out today?

SUE: I hope so. I'll do my best.

TOM: Good. And send a letter of apology with them, will you, please?

SUE: To everyone?

TOM: To everyone who's been kept waiting.

Talking about the dialogue

A

True or false? Correct the false statements.
1 W.W.T. has received many complaints.
2 Sue has answered all the letters of inquiry.
3 W.W.T. hasn't got enough customers yet.
4 Sue hasn't had much help from Mary with the letters.
5 The printer hasn't sent the new brochures yet.
6 Sue will write a letter of apology to everyone.

B

Answer these questions in complete sentences.
1 Why wasn't Tom pleased with the situation?
2 Why was Sue sorry?
3 Why hasn't Mary been able to help Sue with the letters?
4 What else delayed the replies to the inquiries?
5 What does Sue hope she can do?

Practice exercises

A

Tom saw a pile of letters on Sue's desk. She had not replied to them:

TOM: Look at all these letters!

SUE: Yes, I know. I'm **terribly sorry** I haven't replied to them yet.

Working in pairs, comment and apologise in the same way about the following. Use one of these expressions in front of sorry: very, really very, terribly, awfully.

Example: mail—answer
        X: Look at all this mail!
        Y: Yes, I know. I'm **awfully sorry** I haven't answered it yet.
1 mistakes—correct
2 brochures—send out
3 inquiries—deal with
4 correspondence—file
5 letters—open

B

Sue could have apologised to Tom in a different (more formal) way:

TOM: Look at all these letters!

SUE: Yes, I know. I **apologise for not** reply**ing** to them before.

Repeat the comments as in A above, but this time use the more formal form of apology.

Example: mail—answer

    X: Look at all this mail!

    Y: Yes, I know. I **apologise for not** answer**ing** it before.

C

Sue explained why she hadn't been able to cope with all the letters of inquiry. She said:

    "We've had **so many** inquiries **that** I haven't been able to cope with them all."

Working in pairs, ask questions and give explanations like this:

Example (a): You haven't been able to file all the letters yet.

    X: Why haven't you filed all the letters?

    Y: We've had **so many** letters **that** I haven't been able to file them yet.

Example (b): You haven't dealt with all the correspondence.

    X: Why haven't you dealt with all the correspondence?

    Y: We've had **so much** correspondence **that** I haven't been able to deal with it all yet.

1 You haven't replied to all the telegrams yet.
2 You haven't opened all the mail.
3 You haven't dealt with all the requests for information yet.
4 You haven't been able to cope with all the extra work.
5 You haven't been able to study all the new fare schedules yet.

D

Sue also explained why Mary had not helped her much with the letters. She said:

    "Mary hasn't been able to help much with the letters **because** she's been **so** busy on the phone."

Ask for and give explanations using so (much/many).

Example: You've been so busy that you haven't had time to file the correspondence.

    X: Why haven't you filed the correspondence?

    Y: I haven't filed the correspondence **because** I've been **so** busy.

1 You've been so tired that you haven't been able to work faster.
2 You've had so much work to do that you haven't taken your holiday this year.
3 You've had so many inquiries that you've ordered more brochures from the printer.
4 You've had so many phone calls that you haven't opened the mail
5 You've had so many customers that you've stopped advertising.

E

Yesterday Mary answered a lot of telephone calls from people who had not received replies to their inquiries. She apologised and promised immediate action.

MARY: **I'm sorry** we haven't sent you a brochure yet.

CUSTOMER: Can you send me one today?

MARY: Yes, I can. **I'll** send it to you **immediately.**

In the same way, make conversations about the following:
1 prospectus—now—at once
2 catalogue—this week—tomorrow
3 fare schedule—soon—immediately
4 price list—today—this morning

Make similar conversations, using deal with *instead of* send:

Example: x: **I'm sorry** we haven't dealt with your request yet.
　　　　 y: Can you deal with it today?
　　　　 x: Yes, I can. **I'll** deal with it **this afternoon.**

1 inquiry—today—at once
2 complaint—soon—immediately
3 order—this week—without further delay
4 letter—now—this morning

The letters

A

our ref: TS/SD　　　　　　　　　　　　26th February 198-

Dear Mr Au,

Thank you for your letter of 18th February. We greatly regret the delay in sending you a copy of our brochure. We received so many replies to our advertisement that we quickly ran out of stock of the brochure. We have been waiting for new supplies to arrive from the printer. These have now been delivered and we have pleasure in sending you a copy of the brochure.

Yours sincerely,

J. Downing

pp. T. Standish
Sales Manager

Answer these questions in complete sentences.
1　When did Mr Au write to W.W.T.?
2　Why was there a delay in sending him a brochure?
3　Why can W.W.T. send him one now?

B

```
our ref:  TS/SD                          26th February 198-

Dear Miss Chardin,

Thank you for your letter of 20th February.  In response to your
earlier letter, we sent you details of our Seven Day Rail and Coach
tour on 12th February.  We must assume that it has been delayed or
lost in the post.

We have pleasure in sending you a second copy of our brochure and
hope that the tour will meet your requirements.


Yours sincerely,

J. Downing

pp. T. Standish
Sales Manager
```

Answer these questions in complete sentences.
1 Why has Miss Chardin written again?
2 What has probably happened to the first brochure?
3 What do W.W.T. hope?

C

```
our ref:  TS/SD                          26th February 198-


Dear Mr Contziu,

We must apologise for not sending you our brochure, 'Holidays in Britain'
and price list.  Unfortunately, temporary staff shortages have resulted
in mailing delays.

We are now able to send you the information you have requested, and hope
that it will be of interest.


Yours sincerely,

J. Downing

pp. T. Standish
Sales Manager
```

Answer these questions in complete sentences.
1 Why has W.W.T. apologised to Mr Contziu?
2 What reason does W.W.T. give for the delay in sending him a
   brochure?
3 What does W.W.T. hope Mr Contziu will find of interest?

Practice exercises

A
W.W.T. regretted (were sorry about) the delay in sending Mr Au a copy of their brochure. They wrote:

"We **greatly regret** the delay in send**ing** you a copy of our brochure."

Write an apology for the following companies in the same way.
1 Philips Electrical Ltd. have not sent details of their special TV offer.
2 Heinz Foods Ltd. have not sent information about their cookery classes.
3 Office Supplies Ltd. have not answered an inquiry about the IBM 90 electric typewriter.
4 Motor Sport Ltd. have not replied to a request for information about the Mercedes 350 SL saloon.
5 Bargain Stores have not dealt with an inquiry of 18th February.

B
We can express our regrets:

"We **greatly regret** $\left\{ \begin{array}{l} \text{the delay in} \\ \text{not} \end{array} \right\}$ send**ing**..."

Or we can apologise:

"We **apologise for** $\left\{ \begin{array}{l} \text{the delay in} \\ \text{not} \end{array} \right\}$ send**ing**..."

Using the patterns in this table, write apologies for the companies mentioned in A above.

We	do must would like to wish to sincerely	apologise for	the delay in not	sending... replying to... dealing with... answering... forwarding...

Example (a): We **must apologise for not** send**ing** you our brochure and price list.

Example (b): We **sincerely apologise for** the delay in send**ing** you our brochure and price list.

C
An apology is usually followed by an explanation (or excuse).

Example: We **greatly regret** the delay in send**ing** you a copy of our brochure. We received **so many** replies to our advertisement **that** we quickly ran out of stock of the brochure.

In the same way, write apologies with excuses for the following situations. Vary the apologies using patterns from A and B.
1 You did not send a prospectus. You have had many replies. You have not been able to deal with them all promptly.

2 You did not reply to an inquiry of 19th March. You have had many staff away with influenza. You have not been able to deal with inquiries as promptly as usual.
3 You did not send a new price list. There have been many price increases recently. You have had to have a new price list printed.
4 You did not send a brochure. You have been short of staff. You have not been able to answer inquiries by return of post, as usual.

D
Now write apologies and excuses for the same situations as in C above, but in the following way.
We **must apologise for** the delay in send**ing** you a copy of our brochure. We quickly ran out of stock of the brochure **because** we had **so many** replies to our advertisement.

E
After an apology and an excuse we usually state what action we are taking now.

Example (a): **We now have pleasure** in send**ing** you a copy of our brochure.

Example (b): **We are now pleased to** send you a copy of our brochure.

Example (c): **We are now able to** send you a copy of our brochure.

State what action you are now taking in response to the following. For each request/inquiry, make three different statements using patterns (a), (b) and (c) (twelve statements in all).
1 a request for a prospectus
2 an inquiry about a price list
3 a request for details of a cookery course
4 a request for information about charter flights

F
Write letters of apology for each of the situations below, making use of the different patterns practised in this unit. Conclude your letter with a statement from this table.

I			be of interest (to you).
	hope that it	will	interest you.
			meet your requirements.
We			provide the necessary information.

1 John Smith wrote to you on 18th March. He asked for a catalogue of your publications. You could not send him one because your stocks were destroyed in a fire at the warehouse. New supplies have now come from the printer.
2 Margritta Nazaros wrote to you on 12th December. She asked for information about cheap air fares to Greece. You could not send it to her before. You have been waiting for details from the airlines. These have now arrived.
3 Sandra Leung wrote to you for details of your secretarial courses. You could not reply before. You had a lot of your staff away ill.

UNIT 5

Following up inquiries

Tom is talking to Mary about the inquiries they have received.

TOM: Have you heard from that American again?

MARY: Mr Wilson? No, not yet.

TOM: Then I suggest you phone him. Advise him to make an early booking.

MARY: All right.

She phones the Thameside Hotel. The operator connects her to Mr Wilson's room.

WILSON: Hallo. Harry Wilson here.

MARY: Oh, good morning, Mr Wilson. It's Mary Jones from World Wide Travel here. I'm phoning to ask if you've received our brochure.

WILSON: Yes, I have. Thanks.

MARY: The tours are very popular, Mr Wilson, so may I suggest you book as soon as possible?

WILSON: O.K. Why don't I book one now? Let me see. Mmm. There are a lot of different tours. They all look good. Which one do you recommend?

MARY: I suggest the Shakespeare tour. Most people enjoy that one.

WILSON: All right. How about Friday?

MARY: Er . . . Yes. Yes, Friday is fine. We've got just one place left.

WILSON: Excellent.

MARY: The coach leaves from in front of our office at 8.30 a.m.

WILSON: Right.

MARY: But I advise you to be there at least fifteen minutes beforehand. Especially if you want a seat at the front.

WILSON: O.K. I'll be there.

Talking about the dialogue

A

True or false? Correct the false statements.
1 Mr Wilson phoned W.W.T.
2 He was still staying at the Thameside Hotel.
3 He had not received a brochure from W.W.T.
4 He made a booking for the Shakespeare tour.
5 The coach will leave from his hotel at 8.30 a.m.

B

Answer these questions in complete sentences.
1 What did Tom suggest that Mary should do?
2 What reason did Mary give Mr Wilson for phoning him?
3 Why did she suggest that he should book early?
4 Why was Mr Wilson lucky to get a place on the Friday tour?
5 Where will Mr Wilson get on the coach?

Practice exercises

A

Tom often checks up on Mary's work and suggests what she should do:

TOM: Mr Wilson was interested in our Historic Britain tours. Have you phoned him yet?

MARY: No, not yet.

TOM: Then I **suggest you phone** him this morning.

Working in pairs, talk about the following in the same way.
1 Miss Nazaros/ask for/information/cheap air fares—send/today
2 Miss Leung/make/a reservation/Asian Airways—confirm/now
3 Mrs Wilson/want/'Historic Britain' brochure—send/without delay
4 Mr Muller/want/information/Charter Airways—phone/this morning
5 Mr Obuko/ask for/price list—type/today

B

Mary is still learning her job, and Tom often tells her what to say to customers:

WILSON: (*on the phone to Mary*) I'm interested in your Historic Britain tours.

MARY: (*to Tom*) Mr Wilson's interested in our Historic Britain tours.

TOM: **Advise him to** make an early booking.

MARY: (*to Mr Wilson*) **I advise you to** make an early booking, Mr Wilson. The tours are very popular.

Working in threes, make conversations about the following in the same way.
1　Mr Smith/low-priced TV sets—come to the showroom today—in great demand
2　Miss Young/the new IBM 90 electric typewriter—place an order as soon as possible—in short supply
3　Mr Provenzano/cheap flights to Rome—make a reservation early—often fully booked
4　Miss Simpson/cookery courses—enrol now—very popular
5　Mr Muller/Bargain Record Club—join soon—only a limited number of members

C

Compare these two statements:
　(a) I **advise you to make** an early booking.
　(b) I **suggest (that) you make** an early booking.
In B above Mary used pattern (a). In the following conversation she uses pattern (b):

MARY:　I'm phoning to ask if you've received our brochure, Mr Wilson.

WILSON:　Yes, I have. I received it this morning.

MARY:　Oh, good. The Historic Britain tours are very popular, Mr Wilson, so **may I suggest you book** as soon as possible?

Make conversations about the following in the same way.
1　catalogue—low-priced TV sets—in great demand—come to the showroom—as soon as possible
2　circular—new IBM 90 electric typewriter—in short supply—place an order—without delay
3　Charter Airways schedule—cheap flights to Rome—often fully booked—make a reservation—early
4　prospectus—cookery courses—very popular—enrol—soon
5　letter—special offer—ends this week—let us know your requirements—by Friday

D

Mr Wilson asked Mary for her advice:

MARY:　Have you received our brochure yet?

WILSON:　Yes, I have. There are a lot of different tours. Which one do you **recommend**?

MARY:　I **suggest** the Shakespeare tour.

Make conversations about the following in the same way.
1　catalogue—a lot of different sets—the Pye 21 inch
2　circular—many models—the IBM 90
3　prospectus—many interesting courses—the Intensive Six Week Course
4　letter—lots of attractive bargains—the Complete Mozart Symphonies
5　3 air schedules—a lot of flights—the 12.30 on Monday

The letters
A

```
Mr Edward Hope,                          our ref: TS/SD
1 David Street,
Coromandel Valley,
S. Australia 5051                        1st March 198-


Dear Mr Hope,

On 7th February we had the pleasure of sending you details of
our Seven Day Coach and Rail tours.  We hope that you have
found them of interest and look forward to receiving your
instructions.

We should like to advise you to book early on these tours as
places are limited.


Yours sincerely,

S. Downing

pp. T. Standish
Sales Manager
```

Answer these questions in complete sentences.
1   When did W.W.T. first write to Mr Hope?
2   What did they send him then?
3   Why are they writing to him again now?

B

```
Ms Hilary Sargent,                       our ref: TS/SD
c/o Y.W.C.A.,
Bayswater Road,
London N1 5JJ                            1st March 198-


Dear Ms Sargent,

We hope that by now you have received your copy of our
'Historic Britain' brochure, and that you have had an opportunity
to study it.

If any of our tours are of interest to you, may we suggest that
you make early reservations?  Places on each tour are limited,
and we should not like you to be disappointed.


Yours sincerely,

S. Downing

pp. T. Standish
Sales Manager
```

Answer these questions in complete sentences.
1 What did W.W.T. send to Ms Sargent?
2 What do they suggest that she should do?
3 Why are early reservations advisable?

C

Mr Pietre Baretti,   our ref: TS/SD
Via Petrarca 24,
22100 Como,
Italy   1st March 198-

Dear Mr Baretti,

We hope you have received your copy of our brochure,
'Holidays in Britain', sent to you on 7th February, In
case you did not, we are enclosing a duplicate copy.

As these holidays are very popular, it is advisable for
you to make reservations as soon as possible.

Yours sincerely,

S. Downing

pp. T. Standish
Sales Manager

Answer these questions in complete sentences.
1 What did W.W.T. send to Mr Baretti on 7th February?
2 Why are they sending him another copy?
3 What do they suggest that he should do?

Practice exercises

A
W.W.T. sent Ms Sargent details of their tours. They wanted her to make early reservations. They wrote:
   "If any of the tours are of interest to you, **may we suggest that you make** early reservations?"

Use the following notes to write sentences in the same way.
1 special colour TVs offer/place an order soon
2 evening courses/enrol without delay
3 Personal Loan schemes/submit an application as soon as possible
4 Employment Services/send your completed application form by return of post
5 flats to let/send a deposit at your earliest convenience

B

In their letter to Mr Hope, W.W.T. gave him some advice, with a reason for it. They wrote:

"We should like to **advise you to book** early on these tours **as** places are limited."

Write similar statements offering advice with a reason. Use the suggestions from A on page 33 and the following notes:
1   the number of sets is limited
2   the number of places is limited
3   the amount of finance is limited
4   the number of vacancies is limited
5   flats to let are in short supply

C

W.W.T. gave Mr Baretti advice, using the expression *it is advisable to.* They wrote:

"**As** these holidays are very popular, **it is advisable (for you) to make** reservations as soon as possible."

In the same way, give advice to someone in each of the following situations. Give your reason first (As . . .) *and use* it is advisable to.
1   Adult Education College—courses very popular/enrol early
2   Accommodation Bureau—great demand for unfurnished flats/ send a deposit immediately
3   Telephone Company—waiting list for new telephones/apply as soon as possible
4   Public Library—heavy demand for new titles/send in reservation card without delay
5   Housing Loan Association—finance is limited/submit applications without delay

D

Some executives do not dictate letters to their secretaries. They tell the secretary what they want to say and the secretary writes the letters herself.

Write appropriate letters for an executive who gives you the following instructions:
1   "Remind Mr Obuko that we sent him details of our service on 10th March. Advise him to contact us early. Say we can accept only a limited number of new clients." (see letter A)
2   "Write to Mrs Weston. Tell her we hope she's had a look at our new catalogue and suggest that she let us have her requirements as soon as she can. Explain that supplies are limited and we don't want her to be disappointed." (see letter B)
3   "Write to Mr Kawahara. Remind him that we sent our price list on 9th March. Tell him we have very little stock left and advise him to place his order without delay." (see letter C)

UNIT 6

Making reservations

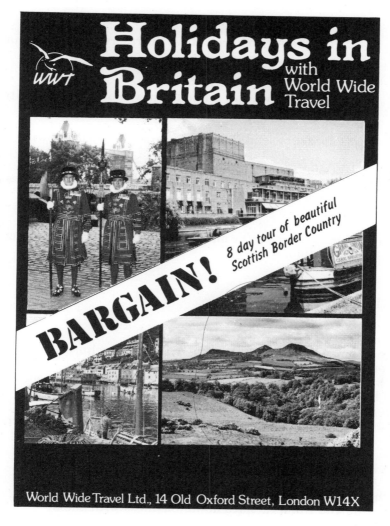

One of the inquiries W.W.T. received was from Mr Blavetsky, the
secretary of the Lions Club of Atlanta. Tom is very interested in this
inquiry because it could result in good business.

W.W.T. sent the Lions Club a brochure, and now Tom is asking Sue if there has been any reply.

TOM: Have you heard anything from the Lions Club of Atlanta?

SUE: Yes. There was a letter in the post this morning, as a matter of fact. They've asked us to make reservations for 43 adults and 6 children on the Border tour.

TOM: Excellent. That should be worth a few pounds! We can do with more business like that. What about a deposit?

SUE: They enclosed a deposit of £50 with their letter.

TOM: Good. What about the names of the people going on the tour?

SUE: They haven't sent them yet. They'll be supplied later.

TOM: Yes, well, there's no hurry. Have the reservations been made yet?

SUE: No, not yet.

TOM: Then let's hope we can make them without any difficulty.

SUE: Oh, I'm sure we can.

TOM: Don't forget to send them a receipt for the deposit, will you?

SUE: No, I won't.

TOM: And tell them we look forward to getting the list of names in due course.

SUE: Right.

TOM: And as soon as you've made the reservations, send a letter of confirmation.

Talking about the dialogue

A

True or false? Correct the false statements.
1   The Lions Club of Atlanta sent W.W.T. a brochure.
2   Tom wanted to do business with the club.
3   The club is organising a Border tour for some of its members.
4   It has sent W.W.T. a list of its members' names.
5   Tom told Sue to ask the Lions Club for a deposit.
6   Sue has already made the reservations for the club members.

B

Answer these questions in complete sentences.

1   Why was Tom pleased about the letter?
2   Why do you think he likes doing business with clubs?
3   What did Mr Blavetsky enclose with his letter?
4   What did Tom tell Sue not to forget?
5   When will she send Mr Blavetsky a letter of confirmation?

UNIT 6

Practice exercises

A

The Lions Club sent a letter to W.W.T. Tom wanted to know if they had also sent a deposit:

TOM: What about a deposit?

SUE: They **enclosed** a deposit (of £50) **with** their letter.

Make short dialogues about the following in the same way.
1   The Grand Hotel sent a letter. They also sent a confirmation slip.
2   Asian Airways sent some tickets. They also sent a receipt.
3   Fastamatic Typewriters sent a machine. They also sent an instruction booklet.
4   The Adult Education College sent their prospectus. They also sent an application form.
5   The Public Library sent their new books list. They also sent a supply of reservation cards.
6   Bargain Stores Ltd. sent their catalogue. They also sent an order form.

B

Tom asked Sue about the names of the people going on the tour:

TOM: What about the names of the people on the tour?

SUE: They'll **be supplied** later.

Working in pairs, make conversations about the following in the same way. Use the verbs supply, send *or* deliver.
1   new typewriter/instruction booklet for/next week
2   photocopying machine/paper for/tomorrow
3   Newbay Holiday Camp/application forms for/in due course
4   Asian Airways/new fare schedule for/as soon as possible
5   our advertisement/photographs for/this afternoon
6   our cheque/receipt for/by return of post
7   our customers/brochures for/on Friday

C

Tom was a little worried about the reservations for the club:

TOM: **Have the reservations been made** yet?

SUE: No, not yet.

TOM: Then let's hope **we can make them** without difficulty.

Working in pairs, and using the information in B above, make similar conversations.

Example:
TOM: **Has the instruction booklet** for the new typewriter **been supplied** yet?

SUE: No, not yet.

TOM: Then let's hope **they supply it** next week.

D

Using the information in B on page 37, make statements like the following:

I am **looking forward to** receiving the instruction booklet for our new typewriter. **Please send** it next week.

The letters
A

9th March 198-

Gentlemen:

      I am pleased to inform you that the Lions Club of Atlanta has chosen your Border tour for part of their tour of Britain in 198-. We shall require reservations for 43 adults (15 doubles, 13 singles) and 6 children under twelve. Names will be supplied at a later date.

      Our deposit of £50 (fifty pounds sterling) is enclosed. Please confirm these reservations at your earliest convenience.

Sincerely yours,

Edward J. Blavetsky

Edward J. Blavetsky
Secretary, Travel Committee

Answer these questions in complete sentences.
1 What was Mr Blavetsky pleased to do?
2 How many reservations did he require?
3 What did he enclose with his letter?

B

8th March 198-

Dear Sir,

      Thank you for your brochure, 'Historic Britain'. I am interested in the Shakespeare tour from June 6th - 13th. Please reserve places on this tour for myself and Mrs Suzuki. I enclose a bank draft for £25 in payment of the deposit.

Yours faithfully,

T. Suzuki

T. Suzuki

Answer these questions in complete sentences.
1 Which tour was Mr Suzuki interested in?
2 How many places did he want reserved for him?
3 What did he enclose with his letter?

C

11th March 198-

Dear Sirs,

        With reference to your Holidays in Britain tours, would you please reserve places on the June 9th - 18th tour to Edinburgh for myself and M. and Mme A. Chardin.

        I enclose my deposit of £20 and look forward to receiving your receipt and confirmation of the reservations.

Yours faithfully,

Simone Chardin

Simone Chardin

Answer these questions in complete sentences.
1 Where did Miss Chardin want to go?
2 Who would accompany her on the tour?
3 What did she expect to receive?

Practice exercises

A

Mr Suzuki wrote:
    "I am interested in the Shakespeare tour from June 6th - 13th. Please **reserve** (two) places on this tour."

Write statements for the following situations in the same way.
1 the publication, 'Today's Secretary'—accept a year's subscription
2 the Heinz Cookery Course—register my name
3 Blackwood Theatre Club season—issue in my name two tickets for each production
4 Moonlight Flight to Rome on Friday 23rd December—reserve four seats
5 Dictionary of Commercial Terms—send me one copy

B

Mr Blavetsky, writing on behalf of the Lions Club wrote:
    "We shall require reservations for 43 adults and 6 children. **Our deposit of £50 is enclosed.**"

Write about the following in the same way.
1 50 tonnes Grade 1 cement—cheque for $2,000
2 six IBM 20 typewriters—draft for $1,250
3 five packets Super Assorted Stamps—postal order for 80p
4 places for 18 students—enrolment forms
5 two economy seats on flight BA914 on 22nd April—full payment of £465

C
Study and compare the following:

.(a) Please { confirm / acknowledge } **receipt of our** { letter. / order. / cheque. / payment. / deposit. / etc. }

(b) Please send your **receipt for** our { cheque. / payment. / deposit. }

(c) We look forward to receiving { your **receipt for** ... / **confirmation of** our ... / **acknowledgement of** our ... }

Write the final sentence in your letters to each of the following, using an appropriate statement from the three examples above.
1 to IBM—you have ordered some typewriters
2 to Charter Airways—you have made some reservations
3 to World Wide Travel—you have sent them a deposit
4 to International Correspondence Schools—you have written to them
5 to the Lions Club—you have written to them and asked to be put on a waiting list of new members
6 to Bargain Stores—you have sent them a cheque for £50

D
Study the following three conversations and then write suitable letters. Pay particular attention to the last exchange in each conversation. As far as possible, model each letter on the one from the letter section referred to in brackets.

1 JOHN: What do you think of the advertisement for Moonlight Flights to Rome?

   MARY: I think it's very interesting. Shall we go on the Alitalia flight on Saturday at 19.40?

   ·JOHN: Yes, why not. That's 18th May. I'll make reservations for us with World Wide Travel, shall I?

   MARY: Yes. They'll need a deposit. You can pay the rest when you collect the tickets.

   JOHN: Right. Well, I'll write to them now.

   ·MARY: Remind them to confirm by return of post.

                                                        (Letter A)

2 MR SMITH: Have you studied that brochure from the Modern Encyclopaedia Company?

   MR JONES: Yes, it's very interesting. You can order one.

   MR SMITH: Shall I send the money?

MR JONES: Yes, send them a cheque. And ask them to supply the books as soon as possible.

MR SMITH: Very well, sir.

(Letter B)

ALAN: The prospectus has come from the Adult Education Centre.

JANE: Oh, good. Is there a Short Story Writing course?

ALAN: Yes, every Monday evening. Oh, and there's another one every Friday evening.

JANE: Monday is better. Let's complete the enrolment forms and send them off.

ALAN: With the money?

JANE: Yes, and ask them to acknowledge receipt of the forms. We want to be sure that they get them.

(Letter C)

UNIT 7

Confirming reservations

Henry Long is the accountant at W.W.T. He is responsible for the company's accounts and all financial matters. Once a week he spends a morning with Tom, during which they discuss customers' accounts and the financial state of the company.

TOM: Have you opened an account for the Lions Club of Atlanta?

HENRY: Yes, and I've credited to the account their deposit of £50. The balance due to us is £560, making a total of £610.

TOM: That's good business from one customer. I'm delighted that we've got this new account.

HENRY: Yes, but be careful, Tom. We can't afford any bad debts, you know.

TOM: Oh, the Lions Club will be safe enough.

HENRY: Maybe, but we can't afford to risk that kind of credit. I advise you to ask for full settlement of the balance due before you issue the tickets.

TOM: I don't want to offend the club, Henry. If they are satisfied with our service this year we'll probably get their business every year.

HENRY: I still think we should deal with them on a cash basis. They haven't asked for credit, so why offer it?

TOM: All right. You've got a point, I suppose.

HENRY: Of course I've got a point. The quicker we receive payment, the better off we are. Don't forget that several customers still owe us money from last year. We need to tighten up our credit control.

42

Talking about the dialogue

A

True or false? Correct the false statements.
1 Henry Long has opened an account for the Lions Club.
2 £560 has been credited to the Lions Club account.
3 The balance due to W.W.T. is £610.
4 Tom doesn't think that the Lions Club will be a bad debt.
5 Henry wants to deal with the Lions Club on a cash basis.
6 Tom will issue tickets to the club before the balance due is paid.

B

Answer these questions in complete sentences.
1 What are Henry's responsibilities at W.W.T.?
2 What doesn't he want Tom to do?
3 Why does Tom want to give the Lions Club credit?
4 Why does Henry want to tighten up W.W.T.'s credit control?
5 What can't W.W.T. afford?

Practice exercises

A

The Lions Club is a new account. Tom said:
   "I'm **delighted that** we've got this new account."

Make similar statements with reference to the following situations.
Use delighted *or* very pleased.
1 Mr Obuko has paid the balance due on his account.
2 Miss Chardin has sent a deposit of £20.
3 Bargain Stores Ltd. will buy on a cash basis.
4 Asian Airways will issue tickets on credit.
5 The total value of the Lions Club business is over £500.
6 Mr Provenzano has sent a cheque in full settlement of his account.

B

The total cost of the tickets (for the Lions Club) is £610. They sent a deposit of £50. Henry worked it out like this:
   The total **cost of** the tickets is £610. We have received a **deposit of** £50. The **balance due to** us is £560.

Make statements in the same way using the information from the following table.

		cost	deposit	balance
cameras	pounds	500	50	450
typewriters	dollars	600	60	540
correspondence course	francs	700	70	630
tour	marks	800	80	720
order	yen	900	90	810
goods	naira	950	95	855

C

Henry Long, the accountant, is telling Tom about W.W.T.'s account with Multinat Ltd., one of their biggest customers.

World Wide Travel Ltd., 14 Old Oxford Street, London W14X, England

In account with: Statement: January 198-

Multinat Ltd.,
269 Baker Street,
London N1 9Y

Date:	Invoice no.	Debit:	Credit:	Balance:
1/1	6894	798.58		798.58
4/1			300.00	498.58
7/1	7324	216.30		714.88
11/1			500.00	214.88
14/1	7989	137.29		352.17
19/1	8008	387.69		739.86
23/1			650.00	189.86

HENRY: On 1st January we **debited their account with £798.58.**
On 4th January we **credited their account with £300.00.**
This left a **balance due to** us **of** £498.58.
On the...

Complete Henry Long's explanation of the Multinat account.

D

Working in pairs, use the information in the Multinat statement of account in C above and ask and answer questions on the lines of the following:

x: **How much** did Multinat still **owe** W.W.T. on 1st January?
Y: They still **owed** £798.58.

x: How much did W.W.T. **receive from** Multinat on 4th January?
Y: They **received** £300.00.

The letters

A

```
our ref: TS/SD/MJ                      17th March 198-

Dear Mr Suzuki,

Thank you for your letter of 8th March 198-, requesting
reservations in the name of Mr and Mrs T. Suzuki on our
Shakespeare tour from 6th May - 13th May.  We are now able
to confirm that these reservations have been made.

We enclose our receipt for your deposit of £25.  We look
forward to receiving the balance due of £96.50.  On receipt
of this balance we will forward your tickets.


Yours sincerely,

M. Jones

pp. T. Standish
Sales Manager
```

Answer these questions in complete sentences.
1 What reservations have been made for Mr Suzuki?
2 What did W.W.T. enclose with their letter?
3 When will W.W.T. issue the tickets?

B

```
our ref: TS/SD/MJ                      17th March 198-

Dear Ms Chardin,

We are delighted that you have chosen our Stratford tour, and
are sure that you will enjoy it.  We are pleased to confirm that
your reservations have been made.

Your deposit of £20 has been credited to your account.  On
receipt of the balance due of £142.75 we will issue your tickets.
We look forward to hearing from you in the near future.


Yours sincerely,

M. Jones

pp. T. Standish
Sales Manager
```

Answer these questions in complete sentences.
1 What has W.W.T. confirmed in their letter to Ms Chardin?
2 What has W.W.T. credited to Ms Chardin's account?
3 What is W.W.T. looking forward to receiving?

C

```
our ref:  TS/SD/MJ                          17th March 198-

Dear Mr Blavetsky,

We have great pleasure in confirming that reservations have been
made for members of the Lions Club as detailed in your letter of
9th March 198-.

Our receipt for your deposit of £25 is enclosed.  We look forward
to receiving the balance due of £585, and a list of names of
club members going on the tour.  Because of the number of people
involved, we must ask you to settle the balance due at least one
month before the date of departure.

Yours sincerely,

M. Jones

pp. T. Standish
Sales Manager
```

Answer these questions in complete sentences.
1 What does the letter to Mr Blavetsky confirm?
2 What is the balance due to W.W.T.?
3 Why must this balance be settled at least one month before the tour departs?

Practice exercises

A
W.W.T. has made reservations for Ms Chardin. They wrote:
"We are pleased to **confirm that** your reservations have been made."

Write similar sentences about the following situations.
1 Bargain Stores have despatched Mrs Smith's order.
2 International Correspondence Schools have accepted Mr Obuko's application.
3 The City Bank has received Mr Nakamura's instructions.
4 The Instant Loan Company has credited Mr Muller's account with $200.
5 The Mail Order Book Company has received a payment of $50 from Miss Wong.
6 W.W.T. has issued Mr Kotasek's tickets.

46

B

Ms Chardin has chosen W.W.T.'s Stratford tour. W.W.T. think that she will enjoy it. They wrote:

"We are **delighted that** you have chosen our Stratford tour, and are **sure that** you will enjoy it."

Write similar sentences about the following situations.
1 Mrs Smith/order/a Sleepwell mattress/find it comfortable
2 Mrs Wilson/accept/the special offer/be pleased with it
3 Mr Obuko/enrol/Advanced English Course/benefit from it
4 Mr Nakamura/open/account/find it useful
5 Mr Muller/take advantage of/Personal Loan Scheme/find it of great assistance

C

W.W.T. will not issue Ms Chardin's tickets until she pays the balance due. W.W.T. wrote:

"**On receipt of** the balance due..., we will issue your tickets."

Write similar sentences about the following situations.
1 Bargain Stores Ltd. cannot despatch Mrs Smith's order: they require her further instructions
2 I.C.S. cannot forward the first lesson to Mr Obuko: they require a $100 fee
3 The City Bank cannot open an account: they require a deposit from Mr Nakamura
4 The Adult Education Centre cannot enrol Mr Obuko: they require his application form
5 The Instant Loan Company cannot credit Mr Muller's account: they require his monthly payment

D

1 Mr Protea wrote to Bargain Stores Ltd. on 8th March. He ordered six cases of Instant Coffee. He sent a part payment of £138. Bargain Stores can supply the order. They will despatch the goods when they receive the balance due of £262.

Write a letter from Bargain Stores Ltd. to Mr Protea in the style of letter A.

2 Miss Teresa Gugic has applied for membership of the English Club. Her application has been accepted. Her entrance fee of $10 has been credited to her account. She will receive her membership card when she sends her annual subscription of $20.

Write a letter from the secretary of the English Club to Miss Gugic in the style of letter B.

3 Mr Alex Scherer wrote to the City Bank on 17th June. He gave outline details of some arrangements that he wanted made and enclosed a cheque for $2,500. The bank requires a further sum of $3,500 and a list of the accounts to be paid on Mr Scherer's behalf.

Write a letter from the City Bank to Mr Scherer in the style of letter C.

UNIT 8

Complaints (1)

26th March 198-

Gentlemen:

With your letter of 17th March, confirming the reservations for the Lions Club members on your Border tour, you enclosed your receipt for a deposit of £25. However, our cheque was made out for £50. I should be obliged if you would amend your records and let me have a receipt for the difference.

Sincerely yours,

Edward J. Blavetsky

Edward J. Blavetsky
Travel Secretary

27th March 198-

Dear Sir,

With reference to your letter of 17th March, I regret to inform you that you have made reservations for my wife and me on the wrong date. You have made reservations from May 6th - May 13th but I requested reservations in June.

I shall be grateful if you will correct the error and confirm by return.

Yours faithfully,

T. Suzuki

T. Suzuki

25th March 198-

Dear Sirs,

I have received your letter of 17th March and am concerned to learn that you have made reservations on the wrong tour. You have booked us on the Stratford tour, but I asked for bookings on the Edinburgh tour. Kindly make the correct bookings and let me have your confirmation by return.

Yours faithfully,

Simone Chardin

Simone Chardin

files: dossier

W.W.T. has received a number of letters of complaint from customers. Sue has taken them into Tom's office to discuss with him.

SUE: I'm very worried about Mary, Tom.

TOM: Oh? Why?

SUE: Well, I gave her some reservations to make and confirm and she's made all sorts of mistakes. The customers are complaining.

TOM: Let me see their letters. (*Sue lets him have them.*)

SUE: I'm very sorry about the letter from Mr Blavetsky. I'm sorry to say that this is the second time we've let him down.

TOM: Sue, this really isn't good enough. You know how important group tours are to us.

SUE: Yes, I do, and I'm very sorry about the error in his receipt. It's my fault, I suppose. I ought to have looked after his reservations myself.

TOM: Why has Mary been so careless?

SUE: I don't know, really. I'm rather worried about her. I don't think her mind is on her job.

TOM: Boyfriend trouble?

SUE: No. Trouble at home, I think.

TOM: Well, she'll have to pull herself together or she'll have to leave. We can't have this sort of carelessness. Let me see the files on all these customers, Sue, and I'll deal with their complaints myself.

SUE: Shall I ask Henry to make out a new receipt for Mr Blavetsky?

TOM: Yes. We must let him have it immediately. But let me check it first.

Talking about the dialogue
A
True or false? Correct the false statements.
1 Mary wants to leave W.W.T.
2 Sue has made many mistakes.
3 Some customers have written letters of complaint.
4 Tom is worried about Mr Blavetsky's complaint.
5 Mary's boyfriend is sorry about her errors.
6 Tom asked Sue to deal with the complaints.

B
Answer these questions in complete sentences.
1 Why did Sue go into Tom's office?
2 What had some customers complained about?
3 Why did Sue say the errors were her fault?
4 What must Mary do? Why?
5 Which files did Tom want to see? Why did he want to see them?

bargain ↑ bonne affaire

Practice exercises

A
Mary has made a lot of mistakes:

SUE: I'm very **worried about** Mary.

TOM: Oh? Why?

SUE: She's made a lot of mistakes.

Working in pairs, make dialogues in the same way.

Example: Some of the brochures are full of errors.
         X: I'm very **worried about** some of the brochures.
         Y: Oh? Why?
         X: They are full of errors.
1   Some of the enrolment forms were sent out late.
2   Some of the receipts have been made out incorrectly.
3   Some of the reservations have not been confirmed.
4   Some of the orders have not been supplied yet.
5   Some of the bargain offers have been wrongly priced.

B
W.W.T. has let down Mr Blavetsky for the second time. Sue said:
"I'm **sorry to say** that this is the second time we've let him down."

Make statements to customers about the following situations, using sorry to *with the verb in brackets.*
1   You cannot supply his order until next week. (tell)
2   The Bargain Offer was discontinued yesterday. (say)
3   A customer must cancel her reservation. (hear)
4   The cheap range of typewriters is sold out. (inform)
5   A customer is not pleased with your service. (learn)

C
There was an error in the receipt W.W.T. sent to Mr Blavetsky. Sue said: "I'm **sorry about** the error in his receipt."

Make statements of apology about the following in the same way.
1   There was a delay in supplying Mr Smith's order.
2   There was a mistake in the 'Historic Britain' brochure.
3   There was an overcharge on Mr Suzuki's bill.
4   There was a misunderstanding over Ms Chardin's reservations.

D
Tom wanted to see the files on all the customers who had complained. He said:
"**Let me see** the files on all these customers."

Mr Blavetsky wanted a new receipt. Tom said to Sue:
"**Let him have** (a new receipt)."

What did Tom say about the following?
1   He wanted details of the overdue accounts.
2   The airline wanted the names of the passengers on flight 902.

3 Tom wants to check all the letters before they are sent off.
4 Mr Chou wants a discount of 10%.
5 Mary wants a day off on Friday.

The letters

A

> 25th March 198-
>
> Dear Sirs,
>
> I have received your letter of 17th March and am concerned to learn that you have made reservations on the wrong tour. You have booked us on the Stratford tour, but I asked for bookings on the Edinburgh tour. Kindly make the correct bookings and let me have your confirmation by return.
>
> Yours faithfully,
>
> *Simone Chardin*
>
> Simone Chardin

Answer these questions in complete sentences.
1 Why is Ms Chardin concerned?
2 What tour did she request reservations on?
3 What does she want W.W.T. to let her have?

B

> 27th March 198-
>
> Dear Sir,
>
> With reference to your letter of 17th March, I regret to inform you that you have made reservations for my wife and me on the wrong date. You have made reservations from May 6th - May 13th but I requested reservations in June.
>
> I shall be grateful if you will correct the error and confirm by return.
>
> Yours faithfully,
>
> *T. Suzuki*
>
> T. Suzuki

Answer these questions in complete sentences.
1 Why has Mr Suzuki written to W.W.T.?
2 When have they made reservations for him?
3 What does he want W.W.T. to do?

to amend : to correct
Application : demande
invoice : facture

C

```
                                        26th March 198-

   Gentlemen:

           With your letter of 17th March, confirming the reservations
   for the Lions Club members on your Border tour, you enclosed your
   receipt for a deposit of £25.  However, our cheque was made out for
   £50.  I should be obliged if you would amend your records and let
   me have a receipt for the difference.


                   Sincerely yours,

                   Edward J. Blavetsky

                   Edward J. Blavetsky
                   Travel Secretary
```

Answer these questions in complete sentences.
1 To which letter does Mr Blavetsky refer?
2 What did W.W.T. enclose with the letter?
3 What was wrong with it?

Practice exercises

A

W.W.T. made reservations for Ms Chardin on the wrong tour. She wrote:
   "I have received your letter of 17th March **and am concerned to learn that** you have made reservations on the wrong tour."

W.W.T. made reservations for Mr Suzuki on the wrong date, thus
   "With reference to your letter of 17th March, **I regret to inform you that** you have made reservations on the wrong date."

Look at this table:

1 I have received 2 With reference to	} your letter of (date)
3 (and) (I) am concerned to learn 4 (and) I regret to inform you	} that you have
5 made reservations on the wrong tour. issued tickets for the wrong date. sent an out-of-date prospectus. not received my application. supplied the wrong goods. made a mistake on your invoice.	

Make sentences from the table by combining 1 + 3 + 5; 1 + 4 + 5; 2 + 3 + 5; 2 + 4 + 5. *Use* I *or* and *in 3 and 4 as necessary.*

Example (a): **I have received** your letter of... **and (I) regret to** ...

Example (b): **With reference to** your letter of... **I am concerned to** ...

B

W.W.T. wrote a letter to Ms Chardin on 17th March. They have made a reservation on the wrong tour. They have made bookings on the Stratford tour. She asked for bookings on the Edinburgh tour. She wrote:

"I have received your letter of 17th March and am concerned to learn that you have made reservations on the wrong tour. **You have booked** us on the Stratford tour, **but I asked for** bookings on the Edinburgh tour."

Write two sentences for each of the following situations. Use either concerned to learn *or* regret to inform you.

1   Bargain Stores Ltd. wrote to you on 25th June.
They have supplied the wrong goods.
They have supplied three cases of soap powder.
You ordered three cases of liquid soap.

2   International Correspondence Schools wrote on 15th May.
They have enclosed an incorrect receipt.
They have made out the receipt for $50.
You sent a cheque for $100.

3   Mail Order Book Stores wrote to you on 14th September.
They have sent you an incorrect statement.
The statement shows a balance due of $168.
You sent a cheque in full payment of the account on 1st April.

Write two sentences for each of the following beginning With reference to.

4   Asian Airways wrote to you on 17th August. (in which)
They enclosed an economy class return ticket to Hong Kong.
They have issued it for the wrong flight.
They have issued it for flight no. AA742 at 19.40.
You asked for flight no. AA700 at 3.45.

5   The Open University wrote to you on 1st July. (in which)
They enclosed an application form for entrance to the University.
They have enclosed the wrong form.
They have sent an application form for admission to a B.A. course.
You asked for an application form for admission to an M.A. course.

C

W.W.T. made the wrong bookings for Ms Chardin. She wrote:
"**Kindly make** the correct bookings."

Request action on the following situations in the same way, using the words in brackets.

1 Bargain Stores have sent the wrong goods. (right)
2 International Correspondence Schools have sent the wrong receipt. (correct)
3 Mail Order Book Stores have sent an incorrect statement. (amended)
4 Asian Airways have issued a ticket for the wrong flight. (correct)
5 The Open University has sent the wrong application form. (correct)

Now request action in the same situations as above, but using

shall
should } be grateful/obliged (*see letters B and* C).

Example (a): **I shall be grateful if you will** make the correct bookings.

Example (b): **I should be obliged if you would** make the correct bookings.

D

Look at the following situations and write letters of complaint, using appropriate patterns.

1 You have received a parcel of books, posted on 12th May.
   They are the wrong books.
   You ordered three copies of 'A Modern Dictionary'.
   You have received three copies of 'The New Dictionary'.
   You want the correct title.

2 You have received a receipt from the Gas Company dated 11th June.
   The receipt shows the wrong amount.
   You sent a cheque for £12.
   The receipt is for £2.
   You want an amended receipt.

3 You have received a statement from your bank for the month of June.
   It contains a serious error.
   You paid in a cheque for £765 on 5th July.
   The bank debited your account by this amount.
   You want it credited to your account.

4 You have received a bill, dated 29th October.
   It contains an overcharge.
   The price of one pair de luxe sheets was £27.
   It has been billed as £72.
   You want the error corrected.

UNIT 9

Correction of errors

Sue has now told Mary about all the complaints and about her talk with Tom. Mary, of course, is very unhappy about what she has done.

MARY: I'm terribly sorry that I made all those mistakes, Sue. Is Tom very angry?

SUE: Well, he's not exactly pleased! As I told you, he's worried that we might lose the Lions Club account.

MARY: Shall I go and apologise to him?

SUE: Why not? It won't do any harm. (*Mary goes into Tom's office.*)

MARY: I'm sorry to disturb you, Tom, but I wanted to apologise for all my mistakes.

TOM: It's a bit late, Mary. They've caused a lot of inconvenience, you know.

MARY: Yes, I know they have. I'm really very sorry about them.

TOM: Yes, well, never mind. We've rectified the errors and apologised to everyone. But you must be more careful in future, Mary. You must keep your mind on your job and pay attention to detail.

MARY: Yes.

TOM: And as I told Sue, I'm very worried about losing the Lions Club account. Americans are very efficient, you know. They don't like doing business with companies that make silly mistakes. Anyway, let's forget about it. I'm sure you'll do better in future.

MARY: I'll try, Tom. And I'm grateful to you for giving me another chance.

TOM: Oh, that's all right. We all make mistakes. The important thing is not to make them too often. Thank you for your apology.

MARY: Thank you for being so understanding.

Talking about the dialogue

A

True or false? Correct the false statements.
1 Tom was not angry with Mary.
2 He was worried about the Lions Club account.
3 Mary apologised to Tom for her mistakes.
4 Tom told Mary to rectify the errors and apologise to the customers.
5 Tom wanted Mary to go and work for an American company.
6 Mary was grateful to Tom.

B

Answer these questions in complete sentences.
1 Why was Mary sorry?
2 Why was Tom worried?
3 Why did Mary go into Tom's office?
4 What did Tom give Mary?
5 What must Mary do in future?

Practice exercises

A

Mary wanted to apologise to Tom for all her mistakes. She had to disturb him. She said:

"I'm **sorry to** disturb you, Tom, **but** I wanted to apologise for all my mistakes."

Make apologetic statements for the following situations in the same way.

1 You need some advice. You have to trouble Mr Smith.
2 There is a telephone call for Mr Jones. You have to interrupt his conversation.
3 Some documents have to be signed. You must detain Mr Smith.
4 There is someone to see Mr Johnson. You have to disturb him.
5 There is an urgent telephone message for Mr Obuko. You have to interrupt his meeting.
6 The line is engaged. You have to keep Mr Wilson waiting.

B

Tom told Sue that he was worried about losing the Lions Club account. To Mary, he said:

"**As I told Sue,** I'm very worried about losing the Lions Club account."

Tell someone about the following in the same way. Begin with As and then repeat your exact words.

1 You told John that the company couldn't afford to lose any customers. (*use* can't)
2 You told Helen that you expected everyone to come to work on time.
3 You told Philip that the company phones must not be used for personal calls.
4 You told Sue that mistakes cost the company money.
5 You told Tom that the errors were not your fault.

C

Agree with the following statements in the same way as the example.

Example: x: You have booked me on the Stratford tour. You have not booked me on the Edinburgh tour.
  y: **As you say,** we have booked you on the Stratford tour, **not** on the Edinburgh tour.

1 The deposit was for £50. It was not for £25.
2 The reservations should be for June. They should not be for May.
3 The balance due is £275. It is not £646.
4 The flight number is BA942. It is not BA902.
5 Our order was for 20 cases. It was not for 40 cases.

Now repeat the above using As you pointed out *instead of As* you say . . .

The letters

A

```
our ref:  TS/SD                                    2nd April 198-

Dear Ms Chardin,

We are so sorry that you have been wrongly booked on the Stratford
tour.  We have now rectified this error and confirm that you are
booked on the Edinburgh tour from 9th - 18th June.

We apologise for causing you this inconvenience.


Yours sincerely,

T. Standish

T. Standish
Sales Manager
```

Answer these questions in complete sentences.
1 Why is W.W.T. sorry?
2 What action has W.W.T. taken?
3 Why has W.W.T. apologised?

B

```
our ref:  TS/SD                                   2nd April 198-

Dear Mr Suzuki,

Thank you for your letter of 27th March pointing out that we have
made a mistake in the date of your booking on our Border tour.  We
deeply regret this clerical error.  It has now been corrected and
we confirm that you are booked from 6th - 13th June.

We apologise for causing you this inconvenience.


Yours sincerely,

T. Standish

T. Standish
Sales Manager
```

Answer these questions in complete sentences.
1 What mistake has W.W.T. made?
2 What kind of error is it?
3 What action has W.W.T. taken?

C

```
our ref:  TS/SD                                  2nd April 198-

Dear Mr Blavetsky,

We are grateful to you for pointing out the error in our receipt
for your deposit.  As you say, it should be for the amount of £50,
not for £25.  We enclose a second receipt for £25 for the
difference.

Please accept our apologies for this error and for causing you
this inconvenience.


Yours sincerely,

T. Standish

T. Standish
Sales Manager
```

Answer these questions in complete sentences.
1 Why is W.W.T. grateful?
2 What is the second receipt for?
3 Why has W.W.T. apologised?

Practice exercises

A

Mr Suzuki wrote to W.W.T. on 27th March. W.W.T. had made a mistake in the date of his booking. He pointed it out to them. W.W.T. replied:

"Thank you for your letter of 27th March **pointing out that** we have made a mistake in the date of your booking..."

Write the first sentence of a suitable reply to the following in the same way.
1 Mr Contziu wrote to Asian Airways on 18th July. They had made an error on his airline ticket. He pointed it out to them.
2 Miss Parsons wrote to the City Bank on 12th August. They had made an incorrect calculation on her statement. She pointed it out to them.
3 Mr Bergstrand wrote to the London School of English on 18th November. They had made a mistake in their receipt for his fee. He drew it to their attention. (drawing to our...)
4 Miss Barbah wrote to Export Shopping Ltd. on 28th June. They had made an error in supplying her order. She informed them about it.
5 Mr Prodea wrote to Bargain Stores Ltd. on 15th December. There was an overcharge on their invoice dated 3rd December. He drew their attention to it.
6 Miss Ritter wrote to Mail Order Records Ltd. on 18th May. One of the records supplied on 12th May was damaged. She informed them about it.

B

W.W.T. expressed their regrets to Mr Suzuki. They said:
  "We deeply regret this clerical error."

They could equally well have said:

We deeply regret	that	you were booked	on the wrong tour.
We are very sorry		we booked you	

*Express regret for the situations described in A. Write an appropri-.
ate statement for each situation.*

Example: To Mr Contziu, one of the following:
  We **deeply regret that** an error was made on your ticket.
  We **are very sorry that** an error was made on your
  ticket.
  We **deeply regret that** we made an error on your ticket.
  We **are very sorry that** we made an error on your ticket.
(*Note:* Not all forms are appropriate to every situation.)

C

Ms Chardin complained that W.W.T. had booked her on the Stratford tour, instead of the Edinburgh tour. W.W.T. replied:
  "**We have now rectified this error and confirm that** you are
  booked on the Edinburgh tour."

Mr Blavetsky complained that W.W.T. had enclosed a receipt for £25
instead of for £50. W.W.T. could have replied:
  "**We have now corrected the error and enclose** our receipt
  for £25, for the difference."

How could companies reply to the following?
1 You have booked me on Asian Airways flight 902, instead of on
   flight 942. Please correct this error and confirm that I am booked
   on flight 942.
2 You have charged me for three cases of soap powder instead of for
   three cases of liquid soap. Please correct the error and enclose a
   credit note for the difference.
3 You have shown a debit balance of $745 on my statement instead
   of a credit balance. Please amend your records and confirm that
   you have done so.
4 You have enrolled me in your Short Story course instead of in
   your Playwriting course. Please correct the error and confirm
   that my enrolment in the Playwriting course has been approved.

D

Reply to the following letters of complaint:

   (a)   refer to the letter and the details of the complaint
   (b)   apologise
   (c)   state what action has been taken
   (d)   apologise for causing inconvenience

1
                                          14th May 198-

I have received your invoice no. 867 of 10th May and am concerned to find that you have charged me $14 for one gross white envelopes, instead of your list price of $12. Kindly correct the error and let me have your credit note by return.

2
                                     23rd August 198-

With reference to your letter of 12th August, I regret to inform you that you have incorrectly recorded my order. I ordered 12 copies of 'A Modern Dictionary', not 21 copies of 'Modern Encyclopedia'. I shall be grateful if you will correct this error and confirm that the right title will be supplied.

3
                                   2nd November 198-

My statement of account with you dated 30th October shows a balance due of $142. This amount was paid by cheque on 12th October. I should be obliged if you would look into the matter and let me know if the cheque was received. If it was, kindly amend your records and send me a revised statement.

Revision

Study this advertisement and write a letter in response to it.

> ## THE WEST END
> ## SCHOOL OF ENGLISH
> Day and Evening Classes
> for Students of English
> as a Foreign Language
>
> Reasonable Rates
>
> Individual or Group Tuition
>
> For free prospectus write to:
>
> The Registrar,
> West End School of English,
> 16 Knightsbridge, London SW1

Reply to the letter of inquiry above.
Enclose a prospectus.

Follow up your letter 2.

Reply to letters 2 and 3.
Send a completed application form for the Intermediate Summer Course from 1st July - 15th July. Enclose a deposit of £50.

Write to the West End School of English.
Complain that you have not received any acknowledgement of your letter 4.

Reply to letter 5.
Apologise. Confirm enrolment on the Intermediate Summer Course from 15th July - 30th July. Enclose a receipt for £25. Ask for the balance due of £150.

Reply to letter 6.
Complain about errors (say what they are) and ask for these to be put right.

Reply to letter 7.
Apologise and make the necessary corrections, etc.

PART TWO

UNIT 11

Inquiries (2)

National Plastics Ltd. is a manufacturing company. It manufactures a wide range of goods made from plastics. Diana Jenkins is the sales manager of the Travel Goods Division. The sales representative is John Williams. Helen Parsons is Diana Jenkins' secretary. She is taking the morning's mail into Diana's office.

DIANA: Ah, come in, Helen.

HELEN: There's a lot of mail this morning.

DIANA: I'm not surprised. I understand from John that there were a lot of people at our stand at the International Travel Exhibition.

HELEN: Yes, so he told me. And some of them were particularly interested in purchasing our range of travel goods. They've written in for more information.

DIANA: Splendid. Can you deal with the inquiries?

HELEN: Most of them. I can send details of discounts and terms of payment. But some of them would like to know if we can send them samples.

DIANA: Mmm. What's their volume of business?

HELEN: They don't really say.

DIANA: Then I'll write to them and find out more about them. We can't send samples to everyone who asks for them.

HELEN: One or two of them would appreciate a visit from John.

DIANA: Good. Pass those letters on to him. He can contact them himself.

Talking about the dialogue

A .

True or false? Correct the false statements.

1 National Plastics Ltd. manufactures travel goods.
2 Diana and Helen are at the International Travel Exhibition.
3 Helen can deal with all the inquiries.
4 National Plastics will supply everyone with samples.
5 Helen will write to the people who John will visit.

B

Answer these questions in complete sentences.
1 Where did National Plastics exhibit some of its goods?
2 Why was there a lot of mail?
3 What will Helen send to the people who wrote letters of inquiry?
4 Why won't Diana send samples to everyone?
5 Why will Helen pass on some of the letters to John Williams?

Practice exercises

A

Replace each question by a statement expressing interest in taking action.

Example: Do you have a wide range of travel goods? (purchase)
I am **interested in** purchasing a wide range of travel goods.
1 Do you have details of discounts and terms of payment? (receive)
2 Do you have any samples of your goods? (examine)
3 Do you have any representatives? (meet one of your)
4 Can I have a credit account with you? (open)
5 Where is your stand at the exhibition? (visit)

B

Express the following inquiries more politely.

Example: Can you send samples?
I would like to **know if** you can send samples.
1 Can you send a representative?
2 Can you accept small orders?
3 Can you supply goods on credit?
4 Can you despatch the goods this month?
5 Can you settle the balance of your account this week?

C

John said to Diana:
"There were a lot of people at our stand..."

Diana said to Helen:
"**I understand from John that** there were a lot of people at our stand."

John made other statements to Diana. How did Diana report them to Helen?
1 There have been a number of complaints.
2 We haven't any catalogues left.
3 I expect Smith & Co. to place a large order next week.
4 Brown & Co. are not a good credit risk.
5 We supplied Robinsons with the wrong goods.

D

One or two of the writers wanted a visit from John (the representative). They expressed themselves politely, using *would appreciate*.

64

Helen told Diana:
"One or two of them **would appreciate** a visit from John."

Helen reported these to Diana in the same way. What did she say?
1   Miss Perri wants an early reply to her letter.
2   Mr Muller wants confirmation of his order by return.
3   Brown & Co. want immediate delivery of their order.
4   Miss Jones wants an interview at your earliest convenience.
5   Robinsons want details of our discounts and terms of payment.
6   National Credit Corp. want early settlement of their account.

The letters

A

Asia Travel Ltd.

14 Patpong Road,
Bangkok, Thailand.

Tel: 910849

Cables: ASTRAV Bangkok

The Sales Manager,
Travel Goods Division,
National Plastics Ltd.,
71 Tenth Avenue,
Harlow,
Essex,
England

our ref: TS/BB/1

Dear Sir,

We understand from the British Embassy here that you are a
leading manufacturer of plastic travel goods. We are interested in
purchasing a quantity of overnight bags and travel document wallets.

Will you please send us your catalogue, with full details
of your export prices. We should appreciate any samples that you
can let us have.

We look forward to having your early reply.

Yours faithfully,

T. Sukwiwat

T. Sukwiwat
Manager

Answer these questions in complete sentences.
1   Who told Asia Travel Ltd. about National Plastics Ltd.?
2   What is Asia Travel interested in purchasing?
3   What should National Plastics send Asia Travel?

B

BARGAIN STORES LTD.

18 HIGH STREET,
EXETER, DEVON

TEL. 897867

The Sales Manager,
National Plastics Ltd.

our ref: LD/ES/JJ   2Oth June 198-

Dear Sir,

      I recently had the pleasure of visiting your display at
the International Travel Exhibition. I was particularly impressed
by your range of lightweight luggage, and would appreciate a visit
by your representative in the near future.

Yours faithfully,

Edwin Simpkins

Edward Simpkins
Senior Buyer
Luggage Department

Answer these questions in complete sentences.

1 Who went to the International Travel Exhibition?
2 What impressed him?
3 What should National Plastics do?

Note: Letter A's opening salutation (p. 65) could also be 'Dear Sir or
Madam', as the sex of the receiver is not known to the writer.

Letter C (p. 67) opens with 'Dear Sirs', as the company in
general is being addressed.

C

Malaysian Travel Services Sdn. Bhd.
598 Jalang Ampang
Kuala Lumpur

Tel: 147625   Telex: MALTAS 61752

National Plastics Ltd.

our ref: AR/JR/1   15th June 198-

Dear Sirs,

        We are a leading travel agent in this city and are frequently
asked by clients to supply them with overnight bags and travel
document wallets. We are considering, therefore, providing such a
service.

        We understand from the British Trade Commission that you
manufacture such goods and we should like to know if you can supply
our requirements. If so, please let us have details of your range of
goods, together with discounts and terms of payments. → Conditions of payment

                Yours faithfully,

                Abdul Rahman

                Abdul Rahman
                Managing Director

Answer these questions in complete sentences.
1 Why are they interested in purchasing travel goods?
2 Where did M.T.S. get their information from?
3 What information do they require from National Plastics?

Practice exercises

limited hability

A
Mr Simpkins recently visited the National Plastics display at the
International Travel Exhibition. He wrote:
    "I recently **had the pleasure of** visiting your display at the
    International Travel Exhibition."

*Write opening statements for letters from the following in the same
way.*
1 Mr Provenzano recently met a representative of Modern Books.
2 Mr Obuko recently visited the showroom of All Colour TV Ltd.
3 Miss Perri recently received a catalogue from Bargain Stores.
4 Mr Rahman recently attended a conference of travel agents.

B

Note the position of such expressions as *last week, in January,* etc.

Example (a): "**In January** I had the pleasure of visiting your display ..."
Example (b): "I had the pleasure of visiting your display ... **in January.**"

Repeat your statements for the situations in A above, substituting a time phrase for recently.

C

Compare: "I **had the pleasure of** meeting ..." (in the past)
"I **shall be pleased to** visit ..." (in the future)

Express the situations in A above as a future pleasure, using pleased to. *Then express the following in the same way.*
1 You hope to receive details of prices and discounts.
2 You hope to send a representative to a customer's office.
3 You hope to attend an interview for the position of clerk.
4 You hope to advise a customer on his requirements.

D

In speaking Mr Rahman would probably have said:
"If you can supply our requirements, let me have details of your range of goods."

In his letter he wrote (more formally):
"... we should like to know **if** you can supply our requirements. **If so,** please let us have details of your range of goods."

Express the following ideas in the same way.
1 If you can supply on credit, let me have details of your terms.
2 If you can produce goods to our design, let us have details of costs.
3 If you can supply the kinds of goods we need, let us have your best delivery date.
4 If you can obtain an import licence for us, let us know your fee for this service.

E

Write letters of inquiry using the following information. Use appropriate patterns from the letters in the letter section above.
1 The Italian Embassy told you about Venetian Glassware Ltd. They manufacture glassware of all kinds. You want to purchase a wide range of wine glasses. You want an illustrated catalogue and details of prices as soon as possible.
2 You visited the Interlangue Ltd. stand at the Frankfurt Book Fair. Their range of dictionaries interested you. You want a catalogue and details of discounts and terms of payment.
3 You are an office equipment supplier. Customers often ask you for a cheap photocopier. An advertisement in the Yellow Pages states that Magic Photocopiers manufacture a low-cost machine. You want to meet their representative.

UNIT 12

Replies to inquiries (2)

Diana Jenkins dictated her replies to Helen, who has typed them out.

HELEN: I've typed all your letters, Diana.

DIANA: You have! Splendid.

HELEN: I wonder if you'd like to sign them now before you go off to lunch.

DIANA: Of course. I'll be delighted to sign them. Well done, Helen. You really are very efficient.

HELEN: Thank you. And would you be interested in buying a ticket for the staff raffle?

DIANA: Ah ha! I knew you were up to something. So that's why you typed my letters so promptly!

69

HELEN: I'm sure you'll be excited by the prizes. There are some super ones. Would you be interested in a cassette recorder, for example? Or a Polaroid camera?

DIANA: I would indeed. All right, I'll buy a couple. How much are they?

HELEN: Fifty p. each.

DIANA: Then I'll just buy one.

Talking about the dialogue

A

True or false? Correct the false statements.
1 Helen has dictated some letters.
2 Diana will be delighted to have lunch with Helen.
3 Helen is an efficient secretary.
4 Helen wants Diana to buy a ticket for the staff raffle.
5 Diana has won a cassette recorder.
6 Diana thinks the raffle tickets are cheap.

B

Answer these questions in complete sentences.
1 What has Helen typed?
2 What does she want Diana to do before she goes off to lunch?
3 Why did she type the letters so promptly?
4 What are two of the prizes in the raffle?
5 In what way does Diana change her mind? Why?

Practice exercises

A

Helen wanted Diana to sign her letters, but she didn't want to sound impatient. So she didn't ask her directly:
"Please sign your letters now."

She asked her indirectly:
"I **wonder if** you'd like to sign your letters now."

Express the following in the same way.
1 Please pay for the goods in advance.
2 Please look at these samples.
3 Please place a small order.
4 Please open a credit account.
5 Please discuss the matter with our representative.
6 Please consider our range of plastic luggage.

Note: **care to** is often used instead of **like to,** for example:
"I wonder if you'd care to see the manager."
See also letter C: "You may care to ..."

B

Helen wanted to know if Diana would buy a raffle ticket. Again, she was a little tentative (hesitant). Instead of saying:
"Do you want to buy a raffle ticket?"

She said:
"Would you be interested in buying a raffle ticket?"

Express the following in the same (tentative) way.
1 Do you want to open a credit account?
2 Do you want to be put on our mailing list?
3 Do you want to see some of our more expensive items?
4 Do you want to work for this company?
5 Do you want to do any overtime this weekend?
6 Do you want to talk to our representative?

C

Study this conversation:

X: Would you be **interested in** supplying our requirements?

Y: We'd be **delighted to** supply your requirements.

Working in pairs, make up dialogues in the same way.
1 visit our factory
2 take advantage of our monthly terms
3 look at some samples
4 have your company name printed on the wallets
5 send us your latest catalogue
6 discuss your requirements with our representative

Note: **pleased to, glad to,** and **happy to** can be used instead of **delighted to.**

Repeat the conversations using these different expressions.

D

Helen did not say:
"The prizes will excite you."

She wanted to stress what Diana would feel, so she said:
"I'm sure you'll be **excited by** the prizes."

Express the following in the same way, using the words in brackets.
1 Our samples will impress you. (by/with)
2 Our service will satisfy you. (with)
3 Our goods will please you. (with)
4 Our designs will delight you. (with)
5 Our low prices will surprise you. (VAT)
6 Our credit terms will interest you. (in)

The letters

A

NATIONAL PLASTICS LIMITED

Travel Goods Division, 71 Tenth Avenue, Harlow, Essex, England
Tel: Harlow 9878643   Telex: TG 8997

The Manager,   our ref: TG/DJ/HP
Asia Travel Ltd.   21st June 198-

Dear Sir,

Thank you for your letter of 14th June, inquiring about our range
of plastic travel goods. We have pleasure in sending you our
latest catalogue and export price list. All prices quoted are
f.o.b. London. Payment is by banker's draft against documents.

We have despatched to you, under separate cover, samples of our
document wallets. The overnight bags are made of the same quality
plastic. The cost of overprinting the name of your company on the
wallets or bags is included in the price of each article. The
mininum order for any article is 200 pieces.

We feel sure that you will be impressed by our samples, and look
forward to supplying your requirements.

Yours faithfully,

Diana Jenkins

D. Jenkins
Sales Manager
Travel Goods Division

Answer these questions in complete sentences.
1   What did National Plastics send to Asia Travel Ltd.?
2   How should Asia Travel Ltd. pay for their orders?
3   What is included in the price of the articles?

B

NATIONAL PLASTICS LIMITED

Travel Goods Division, 71 Tenth Avenue, Harlow, Essex, England
Tel: Harlow 9878643   Telex: TG 8997

```
Edwin Simpkins, Esq.,                    our ref:  TG/DJ/HP
Luggage Department,
Bargain Stores Ltd.                      21st June 198-

Dear Mr Simpkins,

Thank you for your interest in our range of lightweight luggage.
We have passed on your inquiry to our west of England representative,
Mr John Williams, and anticipate that he will contact you shortly.

In the meantime, we are sending you a copy of our illustrated
catalogue and price list.  We can supply most items from stock.

You may find it convenient to take advantage of our monthly terms.
If so, we shall be grateful if you will provide us with banker's
and trade references.

We look forward to being of service to you.


Yours sincerely,
```

Diana Jenkins

```
D. Jenkins
Sales Manager
Travel Goods Division
```

Answer these questions in complete sentences.
1 Who will contact Mr Simpkins?
2 What must Bargain Stores do if they wish to pay monthly?
3 How can most items be supplied?

C

NATIONAL PLASTICS LIMITED

Travel Goods Division, 71 Tenth Avenue, Harlow, Essex, England
Tel: Harlow 9878643   Telex: TG 8997

Mr. Abdul Rahman,   our ref: TC/DJ/HP
Managing Director,
Malaysian Travel Services Sdn Bhd.   21st June 198-

Dear Sir,

We thank you for your letter of inquiry of 15th June 198-, in which
you inform us of your intention to supply your clients with overnight bags and document wallets. We shall be pleased to supply
your requirements.

We enclose our illustrated catalogue and price list. All prices
are f.o.b. London. Payment is by banker's draft against documents.

You may care to take advantage of our printing service. For no
extra charge we shall be pleased to print the name and address of
your company on each article. If you wish to take advantage of
this service, payment must be made in advance by irrevocable letter
of credit.

We look forward to hearing from you.

Yours faithfully,

Diana J-enkins

D. Jenkins
Sales Manager
Travel Goods Division

Answer these questions in complete sentences.
1 How must Malaysia Travel Services pay for their orders if their name is printed on the articles?
2 What may Malaysian Travel Services take advantage of?
3 What additional charges must Malaysian Travel Services pay?

Practice exercises

A

Mr Rahman intends to supply his clients with plastic document wallets. On 15th June he wrote a letter of inquiry to National Plastics, informing them of his intention. National Plastics replied:
"We thank you for your inquiry of 15th June, **in which you inform us of** your intention to supply your clients with plastic document wallets."

Respond to the following in the same way.
Each of the companies wrote a letter of inquiry to National Plastics on 20th June.
1 Power Tools Ltd. plan to wrap their products in plastic sheeting.

2 Food Fair Ltd. propose to supply all fruit and vegetables in plastic bags.
3 The London Library intends to protect all new books with plastic sheeting.
4 Bathrooms Ltd. has decided to offer customers a range of plastic shower curtains.

B

In her reply to Asia Travel, Diana Jenkins wrote:
"Thank you for your letter of 14th June, inquiring about..."

Reply again to the statements in A, using informing us that... *instead of* in which you inform us of...

Example: We thank you for your letter of 14th June, **informing us that** you intend to supply...

C

National Plastics thought it would probably be convenient for Mr Simpkins to settle with them on a monthly basis. They made a tentative offer:
"You **may** find it convenient to take advantage of our monthly terms."

Make tentative offers or suggestions by joining phrases from table 1 to suitable phrases from table 2.

1			2
You may find it	convenient useful helpful necessary advisable difficult preferable	to	take advantage of our monthly terms. discuss your requirements with our representative. obtain the quantities you require. pay by banker's draft. place a small initial order. visit our showroom at your earliest convenience.

D

1 Mr Wilson wrote a letter of inquiry to Speedo Typewriters on 18th August. He would like their representative to demonstrate the Speedo Automatic. Speedo send him an illustrated brochure and price list and arrange for their representative to call. They offer him instalment terms if he has good references.

Express the above information in a letter from Speedo Typewriters to Mr Wilson. Write in the style of letter B.

2 *Rewrite number 1 above in the style of letter A. Make any necessary changes and omissions.*

75

UNIT 13

Placing orders

NEW LINE

Helen is going through the morning post with Diana Jenkins.

HELEN: There are quite a lot of orders this morning.

DIANA: Good. We need them. Business has been very slack this month.

HELEN: Do you want to go through them all or shall I send them down to Invoicing?

DIANA: Is there anything that needs special attention?

HELEN: There's one from Asia Travel. The order is subject to despatch within 60 days.

DIANA: That shouldn't create any problems. The stock situation is good.

HELEN: They want both the wallets and the bags overprinted.

DIANA: Ah, then I'd better deal with that. I'll speak to the people in Production about the order so that there won't be any delays. Anything else?

HELEN: Bargain Stores have placed a large order. Are we prepared to supply them on credit?

DIANA: Have they provided references?

HELEN: Yes. Two.

DIANA: Then hold that order until Accounts have checked them out.

HELEN: Right. That's all. The others are all routine.

Talking about the dialogue

A
True or false? Correct the false statements.
1 National Plastics has more orders than it can cope with.
2 None of the orders needs special attention.
3 Diana is worried about the stock situation.
4 Diana wants to avoid any delays in overprinting Asia Travel's order.
5 National Plastics may supply Bargain Stores on credit.
6 Most of the orders are routine.

B
Answer these questions in complete sentences.
1 Why is Diana pleased with the morning post?
2 What is 'special' about the Asia Travel order?
3 What will Diana talk to Production about?
4 Why won't Diana supply Bargain Stores immediately?
5 Why doesn't she look at all the orders?

Practice exercises

A
Asia Travel placed an order on condition that it was despatched within 60 days. Helen explained this to Diana. She said:
    "The order is **subject to despatch being** within 60 days."

How did she explain the following?
1 Bargain Stores placed an order on condition that it was supplied at 30 days' credit.
2 Asia Travel placed an order on condition that an import licence was granted.
3 The Luggage Centre placed an order on condition that an extra discount of 2½% was given for casn.
4 Jones Quality Products placed an order on condition that any damaged items were replaced without delay.
5 Malaysian Travel Services placed an order on condition that payment made by banker's draft against documents was acceptable.

B

Asia Travel wanted the wallets (to be) overprinted. They wanted the overnight bags (to be) overprinted, too. Helen said:

"Asia Travel want **both** the wallets **and** the overnight bags overprinted."

How did she report the following information to Diana?

1 MARY: The blue wallets are out of stock.
  JANE: The blue bags are out of stock, too.

2 TED: The invoices are all wrong.
  JOHN: The statements are all wrong, too.

3 MARY: Jane has put the export orders in the wrong file.
  JOHN: She's put the export licences in the wrong file, too.

4 TED: Asia Travel has cancelled its order.
  JOHN: Malaysian Travel Services has, too.

5 MARY: Jones Quality Products have provided bank references.
  JANE: They've provided trade references, too.

C

Bargain Stores want to buy on credit. Helen asked Diana:

"Are we **prepared to supply** Bargain Stores on credit?"

How did she ask for instructions concerning the following?·Use the verb in brackets.

1 Malaysian Travel Services want to make payment by banker's draft against documents. (accept)
2 Jones Quality Products want to return five damaged bags. (let)
3 Mr Van Poorter wants to settle his account by instalments. (allow)
4 Pricerite want an extra 2% discount. (consider)
5 Europa Agencies want the goods immediately. (deliver)

D

Diana doesn't want any delays with the Asia Travel order. She will speak to the people in Production about it. She said to Helen:

"I'll speak to the people in Production about the (Asia Travel) order **so that there won't be** any delays."

What did she say to Helen about the following?

1 She wants to know about the stock situation. She will ask the warehouse manager to check the stock.
2 She doesn't want to take any risks. She will ask Accounts to check Bargain Stores references.
3 Asia Travel want to apply for an import licence. She will send them a proforma invoice immediately.
4 She doesn't want Europa Agencies to complain about poor service. She will send them a telegraphic confirmation of their order.
5 She wants Pricerite Stores to place a large order. She will offer them an extra 2½% discount.
6 She doesn't want Asia Travel to delay payment. She will ask them to pay by irrevocable letter of credit.

The letters

A

Asia Travel Ltd.

our ref: TS/BB/2   7th July 198-

Dear Madam,

      Thank you for your prompt reply to our inquiry of 14th
June. We have studied your catalogue and samples and are prepared
to place an initial order as follows:

      400 overnight bags   Cat. Ref. 643 Blue
      800 document wallets Cat. Ref. 942 Blue

Both bags and wallets should be overprinted with the words 'Asia
Travel Ltd.' in gold in the style of your sample. (Cat. Ref. 545)

      This order is subject to despatch being within 60 days of
today's date.

      Government regulations require us to obtain an import
licence for plastic articles. All goods imported against licences
must be paid for in advance by irrevocable letter of credit. We
look forward, therefore, to receiving your proforma invoice as
soon as possible in order that we may attend to the formalities.

      Yours faithfully,

      T. Sukwiwat

      T. Sukwiwat
      Manager

Answer these questions in complete sentences.
1 What have Asia Travel ordered?
2 How do they want the goods overprinted?
3 How will they pay for the goods?

B

BARGAIN STORES LTD.

18 HIGH STREET,
EXETER, DEVON

TEL. 897867

14th June 198-

Dear Ms Jenkins,

        Further to our discussion with your Mr Williams, we are now able to confirm our order for your range of travel goods. Our official order form is enclosed.

        We should like to take advantage of your monthly terms. For information concerning our credit standing please refer to Wilcox & Brown Ltd., 14 Chancery Lane, London, W.C.2, and to the National & Country Bank Ltd., 16 Fore Street, Exeter.

        Please acknowledge receipt of this order.

Yours sincerely,

Edwin Simpkins

Edwin Simpkins
Senior Buyer
Luggage Department

Answer these questions in complete sentences.
1 What is Bargain Stores confirming?
2 How will they pay?
3 How can National Plastics find out about their credit standing?

Note: 'Ms' (in letter B above) is often used when addressing a woman whose marital status is not known by the writer. (Pronunciation: /mɪz/)

C

> ## Malaysian Travel Services Sdn. Bhd.
> ## 598 Jalang Ampang
> ## Kuala Lumpur
>
> ### Tel: 147625   Telex: MALTAS 61752
>
> our ref: AR/JR/2   9th July 198-
>
> Dear Madam,
>
> Thank you for your letter of 21st June and catalogues.
> We are pleased to place a trial order, and enclose your official
> order form. Kindly note that any items that cannot be supplied
> immediately from stock should be cancelled.
>
> We do not wish to take advantage of your printing service
> and we shall pay for the goods by banker's draft on receipt of
> documents.
>
> Yours faithfully,
>
> *Abdul Rahman*
>
> Abdul Rahman
> Managing Director

Answer these questions in complete sentences.
1 What kind of order are Malaysian Travel Services placing?
2 What must be done to items that cannot be supplied from stock?
3 How will M.T.S. pay?

Practice exercises

A
Edwin Simpkins of Bargain Stores gave a verbal order to Mr Williams of National Plastics. He then wrote to National Plastics to confirm the order:

> **"Further to our discussion** with your Mr Williams, **we are now** able to confirm our order for your range of travel goods."

Write statements confirming the following in the same way.
1 Pricerite Ltd. placed a verbal order during a telephone conversation with Mr Jones for 25 filing cabinets.
2 Wilson's Quality Products sent a cable on 18th July ordering one gross of typewriter ribbons.
3 Acme Stores placed an order for a range of packing cases during a discussion with Mr Perri on 12th May.
4 Mr Zwart visited the National Plastics showroom on 19th June and placed a verbal order with one of the representatives for a range of travel goods.

B

Write six sentences (two for each example) placing orders for goods from the following catalogue.

Example (a): We **are prepared to place** an initial order **as follows:**
10 overnight bags Cat. Ref. 812 Green £7.25 each

Example (b): We **are pleased to place** a trial order **as follows:**
20 shoe protectors Cat. Ref. 774 Brown £1.50 pair

Example (c): We **should like to take** advantage of your offer and place an order **as follows:**
100 brief cases Cat. Ref. 218 Black £12.50 each

CAT. REF.	ITEM	PRICE
812	Overnight bags Blue, Green or Gold	£7.25 each
936	Document wallets Blue, Green or Gold	£1.15 each
1004	Portable wardrobes Green or Brown	£8.50 each
1218	Brief cases Brown or Black	£12.50 each
1362	Foldaway raincoats White, Red or Black Sizes 8-15 inclusive	£8.50 each
1774	Shoe protectors Black or Brown Sizes 4-11 inclusive	£1.50 pair

C

Asia Travel had to attend to certain formalities before they could import goods. They required a proforma invoice. They explained the situation and wrote:

"We look forward, therefore, to receiving your proforma invoice **in order that we may** attend to the formalities."

What did the following companies write?

1 Office Buildings Ltd. have to obtain planning permission. They require specifications of the proposed building.
2 Modern Computers Ltd. have to arrange for installation. They require a confirmed order.
3 National Plastics require approximate details of a customer's annual orders. They must plan production.
4 Office Machines Ltd. need full details of the faulty parts. They must obtain replacements from the factory.

D

Use the following notes to write letters placing orders with suitable firms. Use appropriate patterns from the letters above.

1 6 gross typewriter ribbons, black, nylon. Cat. ref. 189. 20 reams typewriter carbon. Cat. ref. 198. Order subject to delivery in 30 days. Monthly terms. 2 credit references provided.
2 Catalogue and price list sent May 28th. Official order form enclosed. Goods not in stock not to be supplied at later date. Extra 2½% discount offer for cash payment not accepted. Payment by banker's draft against documents.

UNIT 14

Establishing credit

Edward Biggin is the credit controller for National Plastics Ltd. He is responsible for making sure that only reliable customers are supplied on credit and that they pay their bills on time. Diana is talking to him about a customer who wishes to be supplied on credit.

DIANA: I've had a letter from Europa Agencies in Paris. They want to place regular orders in future and it will be more convenient for them if they can pay monthly.

EDWARD: Do we know anything about them?

DIANA: Not much. They've placed occasional orders during the past year, but they've always paid cash up to now.

EDWARD: What amount is likely to be involved?

DIANA: They don't say, but not much more than a thousand at any one time, I shouldn't think.

EDWARD: It's a pretty small account.

DIANA: Yes, but it's worth having. I'd be grateful if you'd find out whether they are a good risk for that amount.

EDWARD: All right. Have they provided references?

DIANA: Yes. They've given the Paris branch of the Chase Manhattan Bank and Wilcox & Brown of Burnley as their references.

EDWARD: I'll write off today and let you know as soon as I get a reply. But I'd prefer it, Diana, if we could restrict credit terms to our major customers.

DIANA: Sometimes, Edward, small customers become very big ones. I don't want to risk losing sales.

Talking about the dialogue

A

True or false? Correct the false statements.
1 Europa Agencies want to increase their business with National Plastics.
2 Europa Agencies are a good credit risk.
3 Europa Agencies are one of National Plastics biggest accounts.
4 Europa Agencies have provided two credit references.
5 Edward doesn't want every customer to be supplied on credit.
6 Diana is not interested in small customers.

B

Answer these questions in complete sentences.
1 Why do Europa Agencies want to buy on credit in future?
2 What kind of orders have they placed during the past year?
3 What is the value of their monthly business likely to be?
4 What does Diana want Edward to find out?
5 Why doesn't Diana want to restrict credit facilities to major customers?

Practice exercises

A

Europa Agencies want to buy on credit. A certain amount of money will be involved. Edward wanted to know the probable amount. He asked:
"What amount is **likely to** be involved?"

Ask questions about the following in the same way. Begin with Which *or* What, *as appropriate.*
1 There is a strike in the despatch department. Many orders will be delayed.
2 Asia Travel is going to apply for credit terms. References will be provided.
3 Prices are going to be increased. Several orders will be cancelled.
4 We must give smaller discounts. Quite a few customers will be concerned.
5 Credit control must be improved. Some accounts will be restricted.

B

Europa Agencies provided references. They gave a company and a bank **as** their references.

Make the following into a single sentence using as.
1 Acme Finance will lend National Plastics money. It will be an investment.
2 Asia Travel can retain the balance outstanding on their account for six months. It can be a loan.

3   I enclose a cheque for $90. It is a deposit.
4   Bargain Stores have sent a draft for $3,000. It is part payment of
    their account.
5   Although there are errors in your account we have paid it in full.
    This is a gesture of our good faith.

C

Europa Agencies do not want to pay cash. They want to pay monthly:
>   "**It will be more convenient for them if** they can pay month-
>   ly."

Express the following in the same way.

1   Bargain Stores do not want to take delivery now. They want to
    take delivery next month.
2   Asia Travel do not want to place a large order. They want to place
    a small trial order.
3   Malaysian Travel Services do not want to pay by irrevocable
    letter of credit. They want to pay by banker's draft against
    documents.
4   Discount Stores do not want to settle their account in full. They
    want to settle it in equal monthly instalments.
5   Continental Airlines do not want to pay cash in advance. They
    want to pay cash on delivery.
6   We do not want to supply you on credit. We want to deal with you
    on a cash basis.

D

Edward said to Diana:
>   "**I'd prefer to** restrict credit terms to our major customers."

Express the information in C above, using would prefer.

Example: Europa Agencies do not want to pay cash. They want to
          pay monthly.
          It will be more convenient for them if they can pay
          monthly.
          They **would prefer to** pay monthly.

Now develop short dialogues like these:

x: Which would you prefer? **To pay** cash **or to pay** monthly?
y: **I'd prefer to** pay monthly.

x: Which would be more convenient for you? **To pay** cash **or to
    pay** monthly?
y: **It would be more convenient for me/us** to pay monthly.

85

The letters

A

europa agencies

Place de la Vendome 114, Paris

National Plastics Ltd.   16th August 198-

our ref: Act/PC/21

Dear Sirs,

        During the past year we have made occasional purchases
from your company, but we should now like to place regular orders.
In the past we have dealt with you on a cash basis, but it will
be more convenient for us if future orders can be supplied on
monthly terms. We shall be grateful, therefore, if you will
extend credit facilities to us, and we can offer as references
our bankers, the Chase Manhattan Bank, Paris Branch, and Messrs
Wilcox & Brown Ltd. of Burnley, with whom we have had business
dealings for many years.

        We look forward to receiving your favourable reply.

                        Yours faithfully,

                        Paul Camus.

                        Paul Camus
                        Accountant

Answer these questions in complete sentences.
1 What kind of orders do Europa Agencies want to place in the future?
2 On what terms do they want to be supplied?
3 What have they provided National Plastics with?

B

NATIONAL PLASTICS LIMITED

Travel Goods Division, 71 Tenth Avenue, Harlow, Essex, England
Tel: Harlow 9878643 Telex: TG 8997

The Manager   23rd August 198-
Chase Manhattan Bank,
Paris 5.   our ref: CC/EB/JS

Dear Sir,

Your name has been given to us by Europa Agencies who wish us
to extend to them credit facilities. The amount likely to be
outstanding at any one time is about £3,000 sterling.

We should be grateful if you would let us know whether, in your
opinion, the amount of credit requested is appropriate.

Any information you provide will, of course, be treated in the
strictest confidence.

Yours faithfully,

E Biggin.

Edward Biggin
Credit Controller

Answer these questions in complete sentences.
1   Why did National Plastics write to the Chase Manhatten Bank?
2   How much credit is likely to be involved?
3   What do National Plastics want the bank to tell them?

Note: Compare the arrangements of the two letters. The style of
letter B (no indentation) is probably more usual today, but
the style of letter A (with indentation) is also used.

C

```
                    Chase Manhattan Bank
                            Paris


    Mr Edward Biggin,
    Credit Controller,
    National Plastics Ltd.                    28th August 198-


    Dear Mr Biggin,

                Thank you for your letter of 23rd August.  The
    company you refer to is well established and the account they
    maintain with us has always been properly conducted.  We
    consider it would be appropriate for you to extend credit to
    them for the amount mentioned in your letter.



                    Sincerely yours,

                    Ernest J. Wallace

                    Ernest J. Wallace
                    pp. Manager
```

Answer these questions in complete sentences.
1   In what way has Europa Agencies conducted their account with the bank?
2   What is the bank's opinion of Europa Agencies' credit standing?

D

```
                    Wilcox & Brown Ltd.
                        Burnley


    Mr Edward Biggin,                    our ref: act/JR
    Credit Controller,
    National Plastics Ltd.               28th August 198-


    Dear Sir,

                We regret that we are unable to provide you with information
    concerning the credit standing of the firm mentioned in your letter
    of 23rd August.

                We have done business with them for a number of years, but
    all our dealings with them to date have been on a cash basis.



                    Yours faithfully,

                    Joshua Rowntree

                    Joshua Rowntree
                    Accountant
```

Answer this question in a complete sentence.

Why can't Wilcox & Brown provide any information concerning the credit standing of Europa Agencies?

Practice exercises

A

Europa Agencies wrote:

"**During the past year** we **have made** occasional purchases from your company, but we should now like to place regular orders."

Using the time phrases below, make statements in the same way.

during the past year	until recently	in the past	to date
so far	up till now	for some years	

1   pay cash for our purchases/settle our account monthly
2   charge customers on an f.o.b. basis/issue c.i.f. invoices
3   not take advantage of your printing service/make use of this offer
4   pay by irrevocable letter of credit/pay by banker's draft against documents

B

Imagine that Europa Agencies has requested your company to give them credit up to about £1,000. Obviously, you will *want to know if* they are a reliable company and if the amount (of credit) *which they have requested* is appropriate. You can ask about it like this:

"**Please tell us** if the amount **requested** is appropriate."

Ask about the following in the same way.

1   Asia Travel ordered a quantity of luggage. Ask if the luggage which they ordered is for immediate supply.
2   International Chemicals rendered an account. Ask if the account which they rendered is for immediate payment.
3   Office Supplies Ltd. supplied four new typewriters. Ask if the typewriters which they supplied are the latest model.
4   Bargain Stores mentioned a large order in their letter. Ask if the order which they mentioned in their letter will be placed this month.
5   We delivered a range of goods on Tuesday. Ask if the goods which we delivered are satisfactory.
6   We despatched some samples by air freight. Ask if the samples which we despatched by air freight have arrived safely.

Repeat this exercise using, We should like to know if ... *in place of* Please tell us if ...

C

Edward wanted to know if the amount of credit that had been requested by Europa Agencies was appropriate. Speaking, he would probably have said:

"Is the amount of credit they've requested appropriate?"

In his letter he wrote (more formally):

"We should be grateful if you would let us know **whether** the amount of credit requested is appropriate."

Express the following in the same formal way.
1 Is your order confirmed?
2 Were the goods despatched by air freight?
3 Has the account been paid?
4 Did our representative call?
5 Are our references satisfactory?
6 Will you visit our showroom next month?
7 Have the samples arrived?
8 May we expect to receive your order in the near future?

D

Write letters for the following situations.
1 You are the chief buyer for Bargain Stores. For several years you have been paying for your orders by letter of credit. You now want to pay by banker's draft against documents. Write to your suppliers, requesting this change of method of payment. Supply two references. Each order will be approximately £3,000 in value.
2 Write a letter taking up the references supplied in letter 1.
3 Write two letters in reply to letter 2, one in the style of letter C and one in the style of letter D.

UNIT 15

Acceptance of orders

National Plastics Ltd. have received a number of orders from customers who want to be supplied on credit. These customers' credit references have been checked and National Plastics are now prepared to accept the orders, although they are not prepared to supply all the customers on credit. Diana Jenkins, the sales manager, is talking to Linda Simpson, the senior invoicing clerk, and handing her some correspondence.

DIANA: These orders have to be invoiced, Linda. Will you see to them, please?

LINDA: Yes, of course. I see that they have asked for credit. Has Mr Biggin checked their references?

DIANA: Yes. I'm glad to say we'll be able to extend normal credit terms to Europa Agencies and Continental Airlines.

LINDA: And what about Malaysian Travel Services?

DIANA: No. Mr Biggin thinks we should be careful about them, so we shan't be able to help them at the moment.

LINDA: I see that Continental Airlines want despatch within 15 days. Can we guarantee that?

DIANA: Yes. Unless there are circumstances beyond our control, such as strikes or shipping delays.

LINDA: Right. Should I send a covering letter with the proforma invoice to Malaysian Travel Services?

DIANA: Yes. Will you be able to get the invoices down to the warehouse today, do you think?

LINDA: Yes, I'll do them this morning. Is there anything else?

DIANA: No, that's all for the moment.

Talking about the dialogue

A
True or false? Correct the false statements.
1 National Plastics Ltd. will extend normal credit terms to all their customers.
2 Malaysian Travel Services might not be a good credit risk.
3 Linda will invoice all the orders.
4 She will send a proforma invoice to all customers.

5 National Plastics are not able to guarantee despatch of Continental Airlines' order within fifteen days.
6 Linda will send the invoices to the warehouse without delay.

B
Answer these questions in complete sentences.
1 What did Diana want Linda to do with the orders?
2 To which customers are National Plastics able to extend normal credit terms?
3 Why won't Diana extend credit to Malaysian Travel Services?
4 What circumstances could prevent despatch of the Continental Airlines' order within fifteen days?
5 Why will Linda send a covering letter to Malaysian Travel Services?

Practice exercises

A
Europa Agencies want National Plastics to extend normal credit terms to them. National Plastics can do this.

Example (a): National Plastics **will be able to** extend normal credit terms to them.

Example (b): National Plastics are **pleased to be able** to extend normal credit terms to them.

Make two statements about the following in the same way, using be able to.
1 Continental Airlines want National Plastics to guarantee delivery within fifteen days.
2 Bargain Stores want National Plastics to offer them improved credit terms.
3 Asia Travel want National Plastics to send them. a range of samples.
4 Acme Finance want National Plastics to settle their account in full.
5 Discount Stores want National Plastics to offer them a special price.

B
Malaysian Travel Services want National Plastics to extend normal credit terms to them. National Plastics cannot do this.

Example (a): National Plastics **will not be able to** extend normal credit terms to Malaysian Travel Services.

Example (b): National Plastics **regret that they are unable to** extend normal credit terms to Malaysian Travel Services.

Make two statements about the following in the same way, using not be able to *and* regret unable to.
1 Continental Airlines want National Plastics to offer them a special price.

2　Bargain Stores want National Plastics to despatch their order immediately.

3　Asia Travel want National Plastics to supply them on credit.

4　Acme Finance want National Plastics to settle their account before the due date.

5　Discount Stores want National Plastics to accept the return of damaged stock.

C

Diana asked Edward Biggin about supplying Malaysian Travel Services on credit. Edward was hesitant about it.

Example:

DIANA:　　What about Malaysian Travel Services?

EDWARD:　**I think we should** be careful about supplying them on credit. **I don't think we should** do it.

Make conversations about the following in the same way.

1　Discount Stores—give them special terms?

2　Asia Travel—send them free samples?

3　Continental Airlines—guarantee despatch within 10 days?

4　Bargain Stores—offer them a discount?

5　Office Supplies—accept the return of damaged goods?

D

Linda wanted Diana's advice about sending a covering letter with the proforma invoice to M.T.S. She said:

"**Should I** send a covering letter with the proforma invoice to M.T.S.?"

Ask about the following in the same way.

1　stating the extra discount on the Bargain Stores invoice

2　sending five copies of their invoice to Asia Travel

3　asking the warehouse to pack the Continental Airlines order immediately

4　deleting from all the orders items not in stock

5　invoicing overseas customers f.o.b. or c.i.f.

E

Diana quoted examples of things that were:

"circumstances beyond our control."

We can use *for example* or *such as* to introduce examples:

"... circumstances beyond our control, $\begin{cases} \textbf{for example,} \\ \textbf{such as} \end{cases}$ strikes or ..."

Note the use of commas + *and/or* with more than two examples:

"We can offer you various kinds of accommodation, **such as** houses, flats, bungalows **and/or** two-room maisonettes.

Complete the following statements using such as *followed by any number of suitable examples (but not fewer than the number in brackets).*

1 We should like to receive samples of your products ... (3)
2 We are interested in purchasing office equipment ... (4)
3 We are not responsible for circumstances beyond our control ... (2)
4 We are thinking of purchasing a number of items of new office furniture ... (3)
5 We are looking for experienced office staff ... (2)

The letters

A

NATIONAL PLASTICS LIMITED

Travel Goods Division, 71 Tenth Avenue, Harlow, Essex, England
Tel: Harlow 9878643   Telex: TG 8997

```
Continental Airlines,                     our ref: TG/DJ/LS
Haymarket,
London W.1.                               7th September 198-
```

Dear Sirs,

Thank you for your letter and order of 1st September, reference CA/NP/456. We are pleased to be able to guarantee despatch of the goods within 15 days of the date of your order unless there are circumstances beyond our control, such as strikes or shipping delays.

The goods will be supplied on our normal monthly terms. Payment should be made in full on receipt of our statement.

We hope that the goods will be to your complete satisfaction, and look forward to receiving further orders from you.

Yours faithfully,

L. Simpson

pp. Sales Manager

Answer these questions in complete sentences.

1 What can National Plastics guarantee?
2 How will the goods be supplied?
3 When should payment be made?

B

NATIONAL PLASTICS LIMITED
Travel Goods Division, 71 Tenth Avenue, Harlow, Essex, England
Tel: Harlow 9878643   Telex: TG 8997

Malaysian Travel Services Sdn Bhd.   our ref: TG/DJ/LS

7th September 198-

Dear Sirs,

Thank you for your order, reference AR/JR/3 dated 28th August.
We regret that at this time we are unable to extend to you credit
facilities. Accordingly, we are enclosing our proforma invoice
for the items listed in your order. Payment should be made against
this invoice by banker's draft.

On receipt of your payment, the goods will be despatched to you
within a few days, subject to availability of stock.

Yours faithfully,

L. Simpson

pp. Sales Manager

Answer these questions in complete sentences.
1 What are National Plastics unable to do?
. 2 How should Malaysian Travel Services make payment?
3 When will the Malaysian Travel Services order be despatched?

Practice exercises
A
Study the following conversation.

LINDA: Can we guarantee despatch within 15 days?

DIANA: Yes, if there are no circumstances beyond our control.

In the letter, Linda wrote:
"We are ... able to guarantee despatch of the goods within 15
days ..., **unless** there are circumstances beyond our control ..."

*Express the information in the following conversations in the same
way, using* unless.

1 x: Can we supply them on normal credit terms?
   y: Yes, if the bank does not advise against it.

2 x: Can we extend credit facilities to them?
   y: Yes, if the amount of credit required is not too.great.

3 x: Can we offer them an extra discount?
   y: Yes, if they do not want to take advantage of our monthly
       terms.

95

4 X: Can we accept settlement of their account in instalments?
  Y: Yes, if there are no government regulations prohibiting this form of payment.

5 X: Can we accept the return of damaged goods?
  Y: Yes, if the goods were not damaged after delivery.

Rewrite the above information, beginning your statement with Unless ...
Example: **Unless** there are circumstances beyond our control, we can guarantee despatch within 15 days.

B

National Plastics will despatch the goods to Malaysian Travel Services as soon as they receive payment. They wrote:
   "**On receipt of** your payment, the goods will be despatched to you."

Express the following information in the same way.
1 N.P. will issue a receipt as soon as they receive a cheque.
2 N.P. will issue a credit note when the damaged goods are returned.
3 N.P. will pay the account in full as soon as the goods are delivered.
4 N.P. will resume supplies when the overdue account has been paid.
5 N.P. will release the goods as soon as their bill has been accepted.

C

Look at the example and answer these questions in the same way.
Example: Can you *guarantee despatch* of the goods within 15 days?
   We can **guarantee that** the goods **will be despatched** within 15 days.
1 Can you guarantee settlement of our account within 10 days of receipt of our statement?
2 Can you guarantee delivery of our order without delay?
3 Can you guarantee acceptance of our bill?
4 Can you guarantee removal of the damaged goods within a week?
5 Can you guarantee investigation of our complaint within the month?

D

Write letters of acceptance to the following customers.
1 On 2nd September, Overseas Airlines placed an order, reference OA/NP/267. They requested normal credit terms and provided satisfactory references. They required guaranteed delivery of their order within 30 days.
2 On 3rd September, Wilson's Travel Goods placed an order, reference WTG/NP/981. They requested 30 days' credit and provided references which later proved to be unsatisfactory.

UNIT 16

Complaints (2)

Eight weeks ago, National Plastics changed their employment policy in their warehouse. Since then they have received many letters of complaint from customers, including one from Bargain Stores and a telex from Asia Travel which was followed by a letter. In the following conversation, Diana Jenkins, the sales manager, is talking to Jack White, the warehouse manager.

DIANA: Just look at this list of discrepancies in the Bargain Stores order. It's incredible that anyone could make so many mistakes.

JACK: I know, Diana. But, you see, the staff just don't care. We've had this problem since we changed to temporary staff in the warehouse.

DIANA: And what about this telex from Asia Travel? It's eight weeks since we received their letter of credit and their order still hasn't been despatched.

JACK: We'll have to introduce a new system—or go back to the old one!

DIANA: Is it possible that some of your people are deliberately making these mistakes?

JACK: Oh no. It's just carelessness.

DIANA: Well, it can't go on, Jack. Since we changed the warehouse employment policy we've lost over 50 customers.

JACK: I suggest you take the matter up with the boss. It was his idea: "Employ the minimum number of permanent staff and take on temporaries for the busy period." That was his policy.

DIANA: Well, it's been a disaster.

97

Talking about the dialogue

A

True or false? Correct the false statements.
1 The employment policy in the warehouse has not been a success.
2 Jack White is responsible for this new policy.
3 The warehouse has been employing temporary staff for the past eight weeks.
4 Some of the temporary staff have been deliberately making mistakes.
5 National Plastics has not lost many customers as a result of their employment policy in the warehouse.
6 Diana Jenkins does not agree with this new employment policy.

B

Answer these questions in complete sentences.
1 What does Diana think is incredible?
2 What has been a disaster?
3 Why have so many errors been made in the warehouse?
4 What must Diana do to get the employment policy changed?
5 Give an example of a mistake made by the warehouse staff.

Practice exercises

A

Look at this conversation between two people at Asia Travel:

x: We *sent* a letter of credit to National Plastics *eight weeks ago.*
y: Yes, and **since then we've heard** no more about it.

Reply to the following in a similar way, using since then *and the words in brackets.*
1 The new employment policy was introduced eight weeks ago. (many mistakes)
2 The price list was printed a year ago. (price increases)
3 The Luxor Range of travel goods was put on the market ten years ago. (no design changes)
4 Temporary staff were first employed two months ago. (50 customers)
5 National Plastics introduced new credit terms two years ago. (many bad debts)

B

National Plastics received a letter of credit from Asia Travel eight weeks ago. Notice how Diana stressed the period of time. She said:
"**It's** eight weeks **since we received** a letter of credit from Asia Travel."

Express the following in the same way.
1 We ordered new equipment four months ago.
2 We brought out new designs three years ago.
3 We wrote asking for payment over a month ago.
4 We last had a salary increase a year ago.
5 I asked you to come into my office an hour ago.
6 I dictated those letters to you three days ago.

C

Many mistakes have been made. Diana thinks this is incredible. She said:
"**It's incredible that** so many mistakes have been made."

Express the following in a similar way.
1 No one has complained. (surprising)
2 Orders are coming in very slowly. (disappointing)
3 Many of the experienced staff are leaving. (unfortunate)
4 Some of the mistakes may be deliberate. (possible)
5 We are losing customers. (disastrous)
6 We are letting our customers down. (disgraceful)
7 Some of the new customers are satisfied. (encouraging)
8 We have some permanent staff left. (fortunate)

D

Diana did not like the new employment policy, so Jack made a suggestion:
Example: "I *suggest* you *take* the matter up with the boss."
   Jack **suggested that** Diana **took** the matter up with the boss.

Report what the following people suggested.
1 DIANA (to Jack):   I suggest you increase the amount of supervision.
2 DIANA (to Jack):   I suggest you employ more permanent staff.
3 JACK (to Diana):   I suggest we introduce a new system.
4 DIANA (to Mary):   I suggest you take more care with your work.
5 MARY (to Sue):   I suggest you ask for a salary increase.
6 DIANA (to Mr Biggin): I suggest you check their credit references.

should is often used after *suggested*.
Example: Jack **suggested that** Don **should take** the matter up ...
Repeat the exercise using should.

The letters

A

National Plastics received this telex from Asia Travel on 25th September:

```
8997 TG

61326 ASTRAV

25/9/8-      13.45

D JENKINS

RE OUR ORDER 7/7 + L/C WHY NOT RECD REPLY
OR GOODS SEE CNDITN OF ORDER DSPTCH
WITHIN 30 DAYS

PLS EXPLAIN LETTER FLWS

T SUKWIWAT
```

B

Their following letter arrived three days later:

Asia Travel Ltd.

our ref: TS/BB/2   25th September 198-

Dear Madam,

    With reference to our order of 7th July for 400 overnight bags and 800 document wallets (your proforma invoice no. PF/AT/1), it is now nine weeks since a letter of credit for £3,600 was sent to you. Since then we have received no communication from you; neither have the goods ordered and paid for arrived.

    It was a condition of our order that the goods should be despatched within 30 days of the date of our order.

    Kindly provide by return of airmail post an explanation for the delay in supplying the goods ordered.

Yours faithfully,

T. Sukwiwat

T. Sukwiwat
Manager

Answer these questions in complete sentences.
1   How long is it since Asia Travel sent the letter of credit to N.P.?
2   What have Asia Travel not received?
3   What was a condition of Asia Travel's order?

C

BARGAIN STORES LTD.

18 HIGH STREET,
EXETER, DEVON

TEL. 897867

LD/ES/JJ

1st October 198-

Dear Ms Jenkins,

It is with great regret that I have to inform you that on checking the goods supplied against your invoice 198765, dated 21st September, we have discovered many discrepancies. Goods have been invoiced but not supplied; goods have been invoiced and supplied that were not ordered; and some goods have been supplied but not invoiced. The attached sheet details the discrepancies.

We are returning to you, carriage forward, all the goods not ordered, and hope to receive your amended invoice in due course. The order for goods not yet supplied should be cancelled.

We are most disappointed in the quality of your service.

Yours faithfully,

Edwin Simpkins

Edwin Simpkins
Senior Buyer
Luggage Department

Answer these questions in complete sentences.
1   What does the senior buyer of Bargain Stores regret?
2   What has he returned?
3   What does he want to receive?
4   What must N.P. do about the goods not yet supplied?

Practice exercises

A

When Bargain Stores checked the invoice, they discovered many discrepancies. Their senior buyer wrote:
    "**On checking** the invoice, we discovered many discrepancies."

Report the following in the same way.
1   When you examined the goods, you found many damaged items.
2   When you checked the statement of your account, you noticed many errors.
3   When you placed your order, you made a number of conditions.
4   When you unpacked the crates, you found many items missing.
5   When you reviewed the Asia Travel account, you noted many late payments.

101

B

Bargain Stores informed National Plastics about the discrepancies in the invoice. They wrote very formally:

"**It is with great regret that** we have to inform you that there are discrepancies in your invoice."

Express the following in the same formal way.
1 Many of the goods were damaged.
2 Your account is overdue.
3 We are unable to supply all the goods ordered.
4 There has been a delay in the despatch of your order.
5 We cannot extend credit facilities at this time.

C

Note that we can often avoid repeating the subject (pronoun) and auxiliary verb(s):

Your cheque has been received but ( ) ( ) not ( ) paid into the bank.
Your cheque has been received but *it has* not *been* paid into the bank.

Write out the following (from letter C), putting in the missing words.
(The number of words missing is shown by the number in brackets.)
1 Goods have been invoiced but (2) not (1) supplied.
2 Goods have been invoiced and (3) supplied that were not ordered.
3 Some goods have been supplied but (2) not (1) invoiced.
4 We are returning to you all the goods (2) not ordered.
5 The order for goods (2) not yet (1) supplied should be cancelled.

D

Write letters of complaint to the following:
1 Better Books Ltd.—you ordered 1 copy each of 6 different titles. You have been supplied with 6 copies of 1 title only. You have been invoiced for 60 copies of this title.
2 Speedy Agencies—you received a proforma invoice on 27th October and returned it with a cheque in full payment the next day. The date is now 27th December and you have received neither the goods nor any explanation for the delay in despatch.
3 A company of your own invention—invent suitable details for your complaint.

E

Notice the difference between a telex and a telegram. In a telegram you pay for each word; a short word costs the same as a long one. For a telex, you pay for the time it takes to send the telex, so words are abbreviated where possible (vowels can be omitted more easily than consonants); full stops and unnecessary words are also omitted. Here are some examples of abbreviated (for telex) words:

RE (referring to), L/C (letter of credit), RECD (received), PLS (please), FLWS (follows), SHD (should), WLD (would), TLX (telex), BK (book), CFM (confirm)

Look again at Asia Travel's telex on page 100 and write it out in full, putting in omitted letters, words and punctuation.

UNIT 17

Replies to complaints

Helen Parsons usually deals with the routine correspondence on her own. She replies to routine letters and then takes them into Diana Jenkins for her signature. Sometimes she even signs them on Diana's behalf. However, Helen is an ambitious girl and she wants more responsibility. She is confident that she can do more than just routine work.

HELEN: I'll reply to these complaints, shall I?

DIANA: Er, no. I think I ought to deal with those complaints myself because of their seriousness.

HELEN: I'm quite capable of seeing to them, Diana.

DIANA: I'm not suggesting that you aren't, Helen. It's just that ...

HELEN: I can assure you that I know exactly what to say.

DIANA: They're not just routine complaints, Helen, they're ...

HELEN: That's the whole point! You only give me routine work to do.

DIANA: I'm sorry. But there are some letters I ought to do myself.

HELEN: But why? If I can do them just as well. Look, why don't I prepare a rough draft for you to see?

DIANA: Oh, very well. When can you do them?

HELEN: I may be able to do them before lunch. You won't regret your decision to give me more responsibility, Diana.

DIANA: No? If I give you too much responsibility I shall be out of a job!

Talking about the dialogue

A

True or false? Correct the false statements.

1 Helen has too much responsibility.
2 Diana doesn't think Helen is capable of dealing with the complaints.
3 Not all correspondence is routine.
4 Helen must show Diana all the letters before she sends them out.
5 She will not be able to prepare the drafts before lunch.

B

Answer these questions in complete sentences.
1   Why does Helen want more responsibility?
2   Why did Diana want to reply to the complaints herself?
3   What is Helen's complaint?
4   What does she suggest?
5   Why, do you think, hasn't Diana given Helen more responsibility before?

Practice exercises

A

The complaints were serious. Therefore, Diana thought she ought to deal with them herself. She said:
"I think I ought to deal with those complaints myself **because of** their seriousness."

Express the following in the same way.
1   The matter is urgent. You must deal with it immediately.
2   The order is valuable. You should acknowledge it personally.
3   This customer is important. You should visit him as soon as possible.
4   The problem is complex. You ought to seek advice about it.
5   The situation is serious. You must investigate it yourself.

B

Diana was not sure that Helen knew what to say. Helen assured her that she did.

Example:
DIANA: Do you know what to say? (exactly)
HELEN: I can **assure you that** I know exactly what to say.

Respond to the following using the words in brackets.
1   Will our order be dealt with? (immediately)
2   Is my complaint being investigated? (at this very moment)
3   Is our order receiving your attention? (immediate)
4   Will the errors be rectified? (at once)
5   Will you be able to carry out our instructions? (to the letter)

C

Diana wanted the letters finished quickly. Helen was not sure when she could finish them. She said:
"I **may** be able to do them before lunch."

Note: **be able to** must be used instead of **can** after **may**

Respond to the following in the same way.
1   When can you despatch your order? (this week)
2   When will you receive new stocks? (next month)
3   When can you make a first payment? (on Friday)
4   When will you finish checking the invoices? (today)
5   When can you visit Bargain Stores? (this afternoon)
What did Helen say?
Helen said that she **might** be able to do the letters before lunch.

Report the statements you have just made in the same way, using might *and any suitable subject.*

D

Diana *decided* to give Helen more responsibility. Helen replied:
"You won't regret your **decision** to give me more responsibility."

Respond to the following situations, using the noun corresponding to the verb in italics.

1 Mr Wilkins has *decided* to place a trial order. You appreciate this. (I appreciate . . .)
2 Mr Ahmad has *decided* to cancel his order. You regret this.
3 Mr Sukwiwat has *refused* to settle his account. You are surprised at this.
4 Mr Provenzano *plans* to place further orders. You are interested in this.
5 Mr Obuko *intends* to visit your factory. You are delighted at this.

The letters

A

NATIONAL PLASTICS LIMITED

Travel Goods Division, 71 Tenth Avenue, Harlow, Essex, England
Tel: Harlow 9878643 Telex: TG 8997

Asia Travel Ltd.   1st October 198-

                                      our ref: TG/DJ/HP

Dear Mr Sukwiwat,

Thank you for your letter of 25th September 198-. We are most
concerned to learn that you have not received your order (our
reference PF/AT/1).

A thorough check of our records has revealed that owing to a
clerical error your order was misdirected, together with the
related documents, to Dar-es-Salaam. We are, of course, attempting
to recover the shipment, but appreciate that you cannot be expected
to await its recovery. If you will accept a replacement shipment
we can put it in hand immediately on receipt of your instructions.
You should be able to take delivery by early January.

We deeply regret our error and any inconvenience caused, and we hope
that it will be possible for you to accept a replacement shipment.
If not, we shall, of course, return your payment without delay.

Yours sincerely,

Diana Jenkins

D. Jenkins
Sales Manager

Answer these questions in complete sentences.
1 Why is National Plastics concerned?
2 Why hasn't Asia Travel received its order?
3 What has National Plastics offered to do?

B

NATIONAL PLASTICS LIMITED

Travel Goods Division, 71 Tenth Avenue, Harlow, Essex, England
Tel: Harlow 9878643   Telex: TG 8997

Bargain Stores Ltd.   3rd October 198-

                                                        our ref: TG/DJ/HP

Dear Mr Simpkins,

I am extremely sorry to learn of the discrepancies between your order
and our invoice 198765. Unfortunately the rapid increase in our
business has forced us to employ casual workers in our warehouse.
Their inexperience has recently resulted in a number of errors in
invoicing and packing. We are, however, confident that our staffing
difficulties are of a temporary nature, and that we shall soon return
to our usual high standard of efficiency.

You will, of course, be credited in full for the goods returned, and
our amended invoice is enclosed. The unsupplied balance of your
order has been cancelled, as requested.

We sincerely apologise for any inconvenience caused, and we hope
that we may continue to service your requirements.

Yours sincerely,

Diana Jenkins

D. Jenkins
Sales Manager

Answer these questions in complete sentences.
1 What is Diana Jenkins apologising for?
2 What excuse does she offer for the errors?
3 When does Diana Jenkins expect the National Plastics service to return to normal?
4 What action has been taken and will be taken by National Plastics?

Practice exercises

A
Asia Travel's order was misdirected to Dar-es-Salaam *because of* a clerical error. Helen wrote:
   "**Owing to** a clerical error, your order was misdirected to Dar-es-Salaam."

Express the following in the same way.
1 There have been delays in despatch because of the reorganisation of the warehouse.
2 There will be price increases because of the change in the foreign exchange rate.

3   There is a shortage of goods in stock because of a strike by transport workers.
4   Some orders have been cancelled because of new government regulations.
5   The office is temporarily under-staffed because of the influenza epidemic.

B

Cause and *result* are closely related.

The casual workers in the warehouse were inexperienced.
  This caused
  The result of this was } a number of errors.

Helen wrote to Bargain Stores:
  "Their inexperience has recently **resulted in** a number of errors."

Rewrite the statements in A as results. *Note that* result in *is followed by a noun or a noun phrase (with the* -ing *form of a verb).*

Examples:

A clerical error **resulted in** { **the misdirection of** your order.
                                { your order **being misdirected.**

C

National Plastics regretted their error. They wanted Asia Travel to accept a replacement shipment. They wrote:
  "**We deeply regret** our error and any inconvenience caused, **and we hope** that it will be possible for you to accept a replacement shipment."

Express the following regrets and hopes in the same way.
1   Europa Agencies regret their mistake, etc. They want Fast Rent-a-Cars to continue to do business with them.
2   Office Machines Ltd. regret their oversight, etc. They want Wilson & Co. to return the wrong parts in due course.
3   Profit Investments Inc. regret the delay in replying, etc. They want National Bank to excuse their inefficiency in this instance.
4   Advance Electronics regret the faulty components, etc. They want Power Industries to reconsider cancelling their order.
5   Fly-by-Night Tours regret the late payment on their account. They want Asian Airways to continue to deal with them on a credit basis.

D

1   National Plastics replied to Asia Travel's telex immediately (before they received and replied to the letter). Diana dictated what she wanted to say and Helen sent it off as a telex. Diana dictated as follows:
      We greatly regret that you have not received your order of 7th July. Owing to a clerical error, the goods were wrongly directed. We can despatch a replacement order which you

107

should receive in January. A letter with full details follows.
(a) How did Helen write this as a telex?
(b) Write the same message as a telegram.

2 *Reply to the following letter of complaint. Invent any appropriate explanation.*

F. Wilson & Sons Ltd.,
17 High Street,
Longeaton,
Northampton

The Sales Manager,
Office Machines Ltd.,
12 Broad Street,
London EC4 8WT   25th October 198-

Dear Sir,

On 14th September 198- we ordered five Automat Electric
typewriters, Mark V, at your list price of £467, for immediate
delivery. On 24th October, five weeks after the date of our
order, we received three Automat Mark Vs at your new price of
£523.

We are not prepared to accept part supply of our order;
neither are we prepared to pay the October price for goods
ordered in September for supply in September.

If you cannot supply the balance of our order immediately
and credit us with the difference between the new price and the
old one, we shall return the three machines received, carriage
forward.

Yours faithfully,

H. Brown

Herbert Brown
Purchasing Manager

UNIT 18

Correspondence relating to shipping

Helen Parsons wants to gain experience in all aspects of business and commerce, so she asked for a transfer from the sales department to the purchasing department. She now works for Tom Gooding, who is the purchasing manager.

TOM: I'm afraid you'll find most of the correspondence in this department very routine, Helen.

HELEN: That doesn't matter. It will all be new to me.

TOM: Yes, well, most of it is concerned with shipping. Nearly all our raw materials are imported from the U.S.A. and most of the components we use are manufactured overseas.

HELEN: What sort of components?

TOM: Well, take the luggage department, for example. They manufacture the plastic fabric from imported raw materials. And the locks are all made in Hong Kong and Taiwan.

HELEN: How does the purchasing system work?

TOM: Each of the manufacturing departments has a stores manager. He indents to this department for what he needs and then it's my job to arrange for the requirements to be ordered and supplied.

HELEN: But why doesn't each department order direct from the suppliers?

TOM: Because several different departments may need the same things.

HELEN: I see! The luggage department, which makes cases and bags, might need the same kind of locks as the fancy goods department.

TOM: Exactly. And to enable us to buy materials at the lowest possible price, we buy everything in bulk. That way we benefit from economy of scale.

Talking about the dialogue

A

True or false? Correct the false statements.
1 Helen now works in the purchasing department.
2 National Plastics imports all its products.
3 Tom Gooding decides which raw materials and components to import.
4 Tom arranges the supply of raw materials and components.
5 It is often cheaper to place one large order than several smaller ones.

B

Answer these questions in complete sentencesm
1 Why has Helen asked to be transferred to the purchasing department?
2 Why will she find her new job interesting at first?
3 What does National Plastics import from overseas?
4 Who decides what raw materials and components are needed?
5 Why does National Plastics prefer to buy in bulk?

Practice exercises

A

National Plastics *import* nearly all their raw materials from the U.S.A.
Talking about the materials, Tom Gooding said:
  "Nearly all our raw materials **are imported** from the U.S.A."

Answer these questions, using the passive.
1 What is some luggage made from?
2 How are raw materials and components usually purchased?
3 What are some important letters sealed with?
4 Where is most correspondence kept?
5 Where are some locks manufactured?

B

Tom does not order the raw materials himself: he tells someone else to order them. He arranges for the materials **to be ordered** (by someone else). In the following situations, Helen did not do the jobs herself: she arranged for them **to be done.**

Say what she did in each case, beginning: Helen arranged for . . .
1 Tom wanted some invoices checked.
2 He wanted some flowers sent to his wife.
3 Someone wanted some coffee made.
4 Tom wanted the cleaners to start work after 6 p.m.
5 He wanted some shipping documents collected from the port.

We can express these in another way:
Examples: Tom arranges to have the materials ordered.
        Helen arranged to have the jobs done.

Repeat the exercise, beginning: Helen arranged to have . . .

C

National Plastics want to be able to buy materials at the lowest possible price, so they buy everything in bulk. Tom explained their purpose like this:
    "**To** enable us to buy materials at the lowest possible price, we buy everything in bulk."

Express the following in the same way.
1 We want to reduce our inventory, so we shall not place any further orders for the time being.
2 We want to minimise shipping costs, so we should collate our orders into one monthly shipment.
3 We want to avoid delays in processing stores' requirements, so please make all indents on the forms provided.
4 We want to reduce costs so an attempt should be made to standardise components.

In formal writing, *in order to* is often used instead of just *to*, especially at the beginning of a sentence:
    In order to enable us to buy materials . . .

Repeat the statements above using In order to.

D

The luggage department makes cases and bags. It might need the same kind of locks as the fancy goods department. Helen expressed this information as follows:
    "The luggage department, **which makes cases and bags,** might need the same kind of locks as the fancy goods department."

Express the following in a single sentence. Note that the commas (in writing) indicate a slight pause in speaking.
1 Most of the correspondence was routine. It was concerned with shipping.
2 The raw materials were despatched by sea freight. They were imported from overseas.

3 The store managers are responsible for ordering stock. They have to maintain a daily check on their inventory.
4 The locks are made in Hong Kong and Taiwan. They are an essential part of the product.
5 The sales department is on the fifth floor. It is the busiest department in the company.

The letters

A

Hong Kong Magic Lock Company Ltd.,
7th Floor, Block A,
Kwung Tong Industrial Estate,
Kwung Tong, Kowloon,
Hong Kong

Cables: Lokco   **Tel: 3-618171**

The Manager,   our ref: MZC/PL
Purchasing Department,
National Plastics Ltd.   1st November 198-

Dear Sir,

    Further to your order of 14th September, reference
097856, for 50,000 one metre, brown Magic locks (cat. No. 768) we
are pleased to inform you that the goods have now been despatched
in accordance with your instructions.

    They have been packed in wooden cases, secured with metal
bands, marked N.P.L. London. They are being shipped on board M.V.
Oriental, which sailed from Hong Kong on 30th October, and which
is due to arrive at Liverpool on 29th November.

    A complete set of Bs/L, together with the Commercial
Invoice and Insurance certificate in triplicate have been sent to
the Chartered Bank, Hong Kong, with our draft for $10,000.00 in
accordance with the L/C opened with them. This sum has been paid
by the bank.

    We hope to hear from you in due course that the goods have
reached you safely.

                    Yours faithfully,

                    P.Li

                    P. Li
                    Manager

Answer these questions in complete sentences.
1 What had National Plastics ordered?
2 How have the goods been packed?
3 How are they being shipped?
4 What documents relate to the shipment?

UNIT 18

B

```
                    Marine Agencies Ltd.
                  12 Dock Road, Liverpool

National Plastics Ltd.                    20th November 198-
                                          MAL/JL


Dear Sirs,

        As agents for the South China Shipping Line, we wish to inform
you that on board M.V. Oriental, due to arrive at Liverpool on 29th
November, there are the following goods for your account:

        5 cases:  50,000 Magic locks

        In order to enable us to effect Customs clearance and delivery
of the goods to you, please send the Bill of Lading, properly
endorsed. We shall also require a letter from you to H.M. Customs and
Excise authorising us to act on your behalf.

        If you will let us know the address for delivery, we can
arrange for the cases to be delivered to you as soon as they have
cleared Customs.

                    Yours faithfully,

                    J Lyons

                    pp. Marine Agencies Ltd.
```

Answer these questions in complete sentences.
1 Why have Marine Agencies Ltd. written to National Plastics Ltd.?
2 What do they require from National Plastics Ltd.?

C

NATIONAL PLASTICS LIMITED

Travel Goods Division, 71 Tenth Avenue, Harlow, Essex, England
Tel: Harlow 9878643 Telex: TG 8997

```
H.M. Customs and Excise,              22nd November 198-
Liverpool                             PD/TG/HP

Dear Sirs,

Please accept this letter as our official authorisation for Messrs
Marine Agencies Ltd., of 12 Dock Road, Liverpool, agents for the
South China Shipping Line, to act on our behalf in the matter of
Customs clearance of our shipment on board M.V. Oriental, due to
arrive at Liverpool 29th November.

Yours faithfully,

T. Gooding

T. Gooding
Purchasing Manager
```

Answer this question in a complete sentence.
What does National Plastics' letter to H.M. Customs and Excise authorise Marine Agencies to do?

113

D

NATIONAL PLASTICS LIMITED

Travel Goods Division, 71 Tenth Avenue, Harlow, Essex, England
Tel: Harlow 9878643   Telex: TG 8997

Marine Agencies Ltd.   22nd November 198-
                                               PD/TG/HP

Dear Sirs,

Thank you for your letter of 20th November. We enclose the B/L
relating to the goods on board M.V. Oriental, and a letter to
H.M. Customs and Excise authorising you to act on our behalf in
clearing the consignment through Customs.

The five cases should be delivered to the above address.

Thank you for your assistance in this matter.

Yours faithfully,

T. Gooding

T. Gooding
Purchasing Manager

Enc. 2

Answer these questions in complete sentences.
1   What document have National Plastics sent to Marine Agencies?
2   What instructions have National Plastics given Marine Agencies Ltd.?

E

                          Marine Agencies Ltd.

National Plastics Ltd.   28th November 198-

                                           MAL/JL

Dear Sirs,

        We have received your letter of 22nd November, enclosing
the B/L in connection with the consignment on board M.V. Oriental,
now expected in Liverpool on 1st December. We have also received
your letter to H.M. Customs, authorising us to act on your behalf.
As soon as the vessel arrives, we shall arrange to have the goods
cleared through Customs and delivered to you.

                        Yours faithfully,

                        J Lyons

                        pp. Marine Agencies Ltd.

Answer these questions in complete sentences.
1   What does this letter acknowledge?
2   What additional information does it contain?

Practice exercises

A

Confirm that the following instructions (a) will be (b) are being carried out:

Example: The goods *should be packed* in wooden cases.
    (a) The goods **will be packed** in wooden cases.
    (b) The goods **are being packed** in wooden cases.

1 A complete set of Bs/L together with the Commercial Invoice should be sent to the Chartered Bank.
2 The goods should be despatched in accordance with our instructions.
3 Components should be indented for on the appropriate form.
4 Invoices should be supplied in triplicate, together with the Certificate of Country of Origin.
5 Payment should be made by banker's draft to the International Bank.

B

Now confirm that the same instructions (in A) have been carried out:
Example: The goods **have been packed** in wooden cases.

C

Answer the following questions using due + *to-infinitive (= expected to . . .)*
Example: When will the ship arrive? (29th November)
    The ship is **due to** arrive on 29th November.

1 When will the goods be delivered? (tomorrow)
2 When will the account be settled? (this month)
3 When will the order be processed? (this week)
4 When will the plane leave? (17.40)
5 When will the new manager take over? (first of the month)

D

Use the following notes to write a letter from the Sincere Button Company, Buhkit Timor Road, Singapore to National Plastics, in the style of letter A.

order no. 786453 15th December 198-
1,000 gross stainless steel press-studs, size 4B
cardboard cartons, metal bands
mark N.P.L. London
M.V. Boma Southampton 13th January 198-
Bs/L, commercial invoices, triplicate, certificate Country of Origin, insurance certificate, draft $8,000, Barclays Bank, Singapore

UNIT 19

Reporting errors

National Plastics has taken delivery of the five cases of Magic locks. The cases have been unpacked in the warehouse and the contents checked against the order form and invoice. Unfortunately a deficiency has been discovered. Helen Parsons is discussing it with Tom Gooding, the purchasing manager.

HELEN: The store-keeper has checked the consignment of Magic locks.

TOM: Ah, good. Is everything in order?

HELEN: No. There seems to be a deficiency. They've only supplied 49,000 pieces instead of 50,000.

TOM: There are always errors in consignments from Magic Lock Ltd. I sometimes think they can't count.

HELEN: Perhaps they do it deliberately.

TOM: In the last consignment there were only 98,000 instead of 100,000.

HELEN: Shall I write to them?

TOM: Yes. We can't let them get away with it. Tell them to send us either a bank draft to cover the deficiency or a credit note.

HELEN: Don't you want the other 1,000 pieces?

TOM: No, it's only two per cent of the total order. We can manage without them.

Talking about the dialogue

A

True or false? Correct the false statements.
1 Helen has checked the consignment of locks.
2 The consignment was not in order.
3 Magic Lock Ltd. often make mistakes.
4 The number of locks missing is too small to complain about.
5 Magic Lock must rectify the deficiency by sending 1,000 locks by airmail.
6 National Plastics can manage with 49,000 locks.

B

Answer these questions in complete sentences.
1 Where was the deficiency discovered?
2 What mistake has Magic Lock Ltd. made?
3 How reliable is Magic Lock Ltd.?
4 What doesn't Tom want Magic Lock 'to get away with'?
5 Why doesn't Tom want the other 1,000 locks?

Practice exercises

A

Notice the position of *only*:

Example (a): x: Have they sent 100,000 pieces? (98,000)

y: No, **they've only sent** 98,000.

Reply to the following in the same way, putting only *in front of the main verb.*
1 Have they made many mistakes? (one)
2 Do we owe Magic Lock a lot of money? ($20)
3 Have you finished all the letters? (two of them)
4 Can you work three hours overtime this evening? (1½)
5 Did you take a lot of locks out of stock? (a few)
6 Shall I ask for a refund? (credit note)

In writing, it is safer to put *only* immediately in front of the word it refers to, or the reference may not be clear, for example:
I only borrowed the book.

This could mean: I borrowed it; I didn't buy/steal it.
or: I borrowed the book—nothing else.

Repeat the exercise, putting only *in front of the word(s) it refers to.*

Example (b): y: No, they've supplied **only 98,000.**

B

Compare the following:
Is there an error in the consignment from Magic Lock? (Yes—a lot)
Yes. **There are** a lot of errors in the consignment from Magic Lock.

Reply to the following. Answer Yes *or* No, *using the notes.*
1 Is there a deficiency in the consignment? (Yes—several)
2 Are there many overdue accounts? (No—only one)
3 Is there a lot of stock? (No—not much)
4 Are all the documents here? (No—some missing)
5 Is there a mistake in this account? (Yes—a lot)
6 Is there a list of the contents with the consignment? (Yes—a packing list)

C

The store-keeper says there is a deficiency in the Magic Lock consignment. Helen is puzzled. She said:
"**There seems to be** a deficiency (in the consignment)."

What did she say about the following?
1 Linda has found a mistake in the invoice.
2 A problem has been reported in the warehouse.
3 An overdue balance has been pointed out in our account.
4 An oversight has been discovered in our order.
5 Edward says there is a discrepancy in the accounts.
6 A fault has been discovered in the computer.

The letter

NATIONAL PLASTICS LIMITED

Travel Goods Division, 71 Tenth Avenue, Harlow, Essex, England
Tel: Harlow 9878643 Telex: TG 8997

Hong Kong Magic Lock Co. Ltd.   14th December 198-

Dear Sirs,

We are pleased to inform you that we have now taken delivery of
five cases, one metre, brown Magic locks, as per our order 097856
of 14th September, and found the goods to be in satisfactory
condition.

However, our order was for 50,000 pieces, and you have charged us
and we have paid for 50,000 pieces, but on checking the contents
of the cases, we were able to find only 49,000 pieces. There seems
to be a shortage of 1,000 pieces.

We shall be grateful if you will either send us a bank draft to
cover the value of the deficiency, or issue a credit note in our
favour.

We regret that there appears to be a lack of supervision in your
packing department. This is the fifth time we have had to report
deficiencies to you.

Yours faithfully,

T. Gooding

T. Gooding
Purchasing Manager

Answer these questions in complete sentences.
1 What has been delivered to National Plastics?
2 In what condition were the goods?
3 What deficiency has National Plastics discovered?
4 What action do they want Magic Lock Co. Ltd. to take?
5 Why is National Plastics particularly concerned about the
   deficiency?

Practice exercises

A

Magic Lock did not supply 50,000 locks. They supplied 49,000.
Magic Lock supplied 49,000 locks **instead of** 50,000.

Make statements about the following in the same way.
1 Europa Agencies did not pack the goods in cases. They packed
   them in cartons.
2 National Plastics do not want a refund. They want a credit note.
3 Helen did not reply to the complaint by letter. She replied by
   telegram.

4   Tom will not place further orders with Magic Lock. He will place them with Unilock.
5   Most of National Plastics' customers do not ask for credit. They ask for a discount.

B

National Plastics wanted **either** a bank draft **or** a credit note from Magic Lock Co. Ltd. Helen wrote:
   "We shall be grateful if you will **either** send us a bank draft . . . , **or** issue a credit note in our favour."

Request action on the following in the same way.
1   send a range of samples/ask your representative to call
2   grant us 30 days credit/allow us an extra 2½% discount
3   settle your account/return the goods forthwith
4   despatch the goods within 7 days/cancel our order
5   open a letter of credit/accept a sight draft

C

National Plastics have noticed a lack of supervision in Magic Lock's packing department. They mentioned this to Magic Lock Co. Ltd.:
   "We **regret that there appears to be** a lack of supervision in your packing department."

Mention the following in the same formal way.
1   water damage to the contents of the cases
2   a misprint in a catalogue
3   an oversight in the accounts department
4   a computer error in the stock list
5   an overcharge on an invoice

D

Write a letter as from Bargain Stores Ltd. to National Plastics Ltd.
(a)   acknowledge delivery of your order 8796 of 15th December
(b)   confirm the satisfactory condition of the goods
(c)   point out that there is a shortage: 5 gross overnight bags have been supplied instead of 6 gross
(d)   request that the balance of the order be supplied or the order cancelled and the goods supplied accepted for return
(e)   point out that there are frequently shortages or invoicing errors

E

Write a letter to an imaginary company.
(a)   report water damage to a consignment of goods sent by sea freight
(b)   give details of the order and the nature of the damage
(c)   point out that inferior packing is probably responsible for the damage
(d)   remind the company that you have complained about poor packing many times in the past

UNIT 20

Requests and demands for payment

```
61326   ASTRAV

8997    TG

14/11/8-      11.00

T SUKWIWAT

KINDLY REMIT STERLING 1500 NOW 2 MONTHS
OVERDUE

BIGGIN
```

Helen Parsons has transferred from the purchasing department to the accounts department. She is now the personal assistant (P.A.) to Edward Biggin, the credit controller. She is discussing with him the overdue accounts.

EDWARD: Who owes us the most money?

HELEN: Europa Agencies. They owe £4,000.

EDWARD: How many days overdue is it?

HELEN: Just a month.

EDWARD: Well, I can't remember having trouble with them before. They've probably overlooked it. Send them a polite reminder. Who's next?

HELEN: Asia Travel. They're two months overdue, and they owe £1,500.

EDWARD: Mmm. They usually pay on time, but some of these travel agencies can go out of business overnight. We must insist on immediate payment. Send a short but strongly worded letter. No. Send a telegram and follow it up with a letter. Next?

HELEN: International Bargain Stores, Harrogate. They owe £750 and they are three months overdue. We've sent them three statements and written to them twice.

EDWARD: What's their past payment record like?

HELEN: I don't know. This seems to be a new file.

121

EDWARD: Then look up the old file. Find out whether they've paid promptly or not in the past. If they haven't, threaten to take legal action.

HELEN: All right. And that's all.

EDWARD: Only three overdue accounts? That's not bad, is it, out of over three hundred?

Talking about the dialogue

A

True or false? Correct the false statements.
1 National Plastics owe a lot of money.
2 National Plastics have many customers who do not pay their bills on time.
3 Edward Biggin will write to the customers himself.
4 Helen will send a telegram to all the overdue accounts.
5 Europa Agencies often pay their account late.
6 National Plastics will take legal action against International Bargain Stores.

B

Answer these questions in complete sentences.
1 What is Helen's new job?
2 Why isn't Edward Biggin worried about the Europa Agencies' account?
3 Why has he decided to cable Asia Travel?
4 Which of the three accounts is most overdue?
5 What must Helen find out before she writes to International Bargain Stores?

Practice exercises

A

Helen spoke to Edward Biggin about the Asia Travel account. She said:
"They are two months **overdue**." (meaning: They are two months late in paying their account.)

Compare:
Their account should have been paid two months ago.
It was **due** (to be paid) two months ago.
It is now (two months) **overdue**.

Make statements about the following, using overdue *with a period of time.*
1 The shipment has not arrived. It should have arrived two weeks ago.
2 The bus has not come yet. It should have come half an hour ago.
3 The account has not been paid. It should have been paid a month ago.
4 The aircraft has not arrived. It should have arrived an hour ago.
5 My salary cheque has not come. It should have come a week ago.

B

Edward spoke about the Europa Agencies' account. He said:
  "They've probably **overlooked** it."

*Find out and discuss the meaning of the following words beginning
with over-. Then use them in sentences of your own.*
  Verbs: overlook, overcharge, overpay, overtake, overwork,
       overestimate
  Nouns: overdraft, oversight, overtime
  Adjectives/Adverbs: overseas, overnight

C

Edward wanted Asia Travel to pay their account immediately. He
was very firm, and said:
  "We must **insist on** immediate payment of their account."

*Add a statement to each of the following insisting on action. Use the
noun corresponding to the verb in italics, with the preposition in
brackets. Make any other necessary changes.*
1 I want Europa Agencies to *explain* the delay. (of)
2 I want this typewriter *replaced*. (for)
3 I want this account *settled* without delay. (of)
4 I want the consignment *shipped* immediately. (of)
5 I want the reservations *cancelled*. (of)

The letters

A

NATIONAL PLASTICS LIMITED

Travel Goods Division, 71 Tenth Avenue, Harlow, Essex, England
Tel: Harlow 9878643 Telex: TG 8997

Europa Agencies   TG/EB/HP
Place de la Vendome, 114
Paris, France   14th January 198-

Dear Sirs,

As you know, we are able to grant credit facilities to customers
only on the condition that monthly accounts are paid in full
on receipt of statement.

Payment of your account is now one month overdue. As you have always
paid your account promptly in the past, we are sure that on this
occasion you have simply overlooked the matter.

We enclose a copy of your statement and look forward to receiving
your cheque in full settlement in the very near future.

Yours faithfully,

Helen Parsons

pp. Edward Biggin
Credit Controller

In due course, National Plastics received the following reply from Europa Agencies.

B

Dear Sir,

I must apologise for the delay in settling our account with you. I have been abroad for several weeks and it was not until my return that your account was brought to my attention.

I enclose a bank draft for £4,000 in full settlement.

Yours faithfully,

Helmut Berger

Helmut Berger
Managing Director

Answer these questions in complete sentences.
1 How would you describe the tone of letter A? (i.e. was it friendly, firm, polite, formal, etc.?) Pick out some sentences/expressions to support your answer.
2 What reason did the Managing Director of Europa Agencies give for the delayed payment?

C

NATIONAL PLASTICS LIMITED
Travel Goods Division, 71 Tenth Avenue, Harlow, Essex, England
Tel: Harlow 9878643   Telex: TG 8997

Asia Travel Ltd.,   TG/EB/HP
14 Patpong Road,
Bangkok,
Thailand   14th January 198-

Dear Sirs,

We greatly regret that we have not received a reply to our letter of 1st December or your cheque in payment of your account for £1,500.

We cabled you today, as follows:

KINDLY REMIT STERLING 1500 NOW 2 MONTHS OVERDUE

Unless you have any reasonable grounds for not settling your account in full, we must insist on immediate payment.

Yours faithfully,

Helen Parsons

pp. Edward Biggin
Credit Controller

In due course, National Plastics received the following reply from Asia Travel.

D

Dear Sir,

> With reference to your letter and telegram of 14th January requesting payment of our account, kindly note that we paid this amount on 9th January. The cheque number was 2702496, drawn on our account with the Bank of Commerce, Chancery Lane, London.

> Kindly examine your records, and confirm whether or not this payment has now been received.

Yours faithfully,

T. Sukwiwat

T. Sukwiwat
Manager

Answer these questions in complete sentences.
1 How would you describe the tone of letter C? Pick out one or two expressions to support your answer.
2 What was the purpose of sending a cable to Asia Travel?
3 What was Asia Travel's response to the letter requesting immediate payment?

E

NATIONAL PLASTICS LIMITED
Travel Goods Division, 71 Tenth Avenue, Harlow, Essex, England
Tel: Harlow 9878643 Telex: TG 8997

International Bargain Stores,
45 Market Street,
Harrogate,
Yorks

TG/EB/HP

14th January 198-

Dear Sirs,

Your account with us for £750 is now three months overdue. We have submitted our statement to you three times, and written to you twice. You have ignored all our communications.

It is with the greatest regret, therefore, that we have to inform you that unless we receive full settlement of this account within 7 days, the collection of the amount due will be placed in the hands of our solicitors.

Yours faithfully,

Helen Parsons

pp. Edward Biggin
Credit Controller

In due course, National Plastics received the following reply from International Bargain Stores.

F

```
Dear Sir,

        Thank you for your letter of 14th January.  We greatly
regret the delay in settling our account with you.  Unfortunately,
our cash situation has been seriously affected by adverse trading
conditions resulting from the current economic recession.

        We are optimistic, however, that the situation will
improve, and will be grateful for your patience in this matter.
We hope you will accept the enclosed cheque for £50 in part
payment of our account.  We shall do our best to settle the
balance as soon as possible.


                        Yours faithfully,

                        Linda Johnson

                        L. Johnson
                        Manager
```

Answer these questions in complete sentences.
1 Why did National Plastics threaten to place collection in the hands of a solicitor in their letter to International Bargain Stores?
2 What do you think the letter from International Bargain Stores really means? (i.e. What does it imply?)

Practice exercises

A
National Plastics told I.B.S.:
"**It is with the greatest regret that** we have to inform you that the collection of the amount due will be placed in the hands of our solicitors."

Compare:
(a) informal: We are sorry to tell you that the ...
(b) formal: We regret that we must tell/inform you that the ...
(c) very } It is regretted that we have to inform you that the ...
(d) formal: } It is with the greatest regret that we have to inform you that the ...

Express each of the following in the two ways indicated.
1 advise you—shipment delayed—two weeks (a) and (b)
2 inform you—credit facilities—no longer available (a) and (c)
3 tell you—unable to supply—your order No. 8976 (b) and (d)
4 advise you—insurance policy No. 6745—lapsed on 12th May last (a) and (d)
5 inform you—your services—no longer required (b) and (c)

B

Helmut Berger was away from his office for several weeks. The National Plastics account was *not brought* to his attention *until* he returned. He emphasised his excuse for not paying (i.e. the fact that he had only just seen the account) by saying:

"**It was not until** I returned **that** the account was brought to my attention."

Emphasise the excuse in the following in the same way, beginning with It...:

1 The faulty components did not become apparent until the machine was put into operation.
2 The errors were not discovered until the accounts were audited.
3 The damage could not be estimated until the goods were unpacked.
4 Supplies could not be resumed until your account was paid in full.
5 Your invoices could not be paid until they had been checked against the contents of the consignment.

C

Asia Travel asked N.P. to find out and confirm *whether* their payment had been received or (*whether* it had) *not* (been received). They wrote:

"... and confirm **whether or not** this payment has now been received."

Look at the following questions and respond using whether or not:

Example: Has the account been paid?
          Find out **whether or not** the account has been paid.

1 Do they usually pay on time?
2 Have the goods been unpacked yet?
3 Have the cases been loaded on to the ship yet?
4 Is the M.V. Oriental a container ship?
5 Will National Plastics accept part payment of their account?

D

Telegrams

National Plastics cabled Asia Travel (see letter C) in an attempt to impress on them the urgency of the situation. The following is a cabled version of letter A:

CREDIT AVAILABLE ONLY IF MONTHLY ACCOUNTS PAID ON RECEIPT STOP FEEL YOU HAVE OVERLOOKED LAST STATEMENT STOP GRATEFUL FOR SETTLEMENT SOONEST.

Express the contents of letters B, D and E in the form of cables.

E

Write three different letters requesting payment of overdue accounts.
The first should be a polite reminder; the second a strong request for payment; and the third should threaten legal action.

Reply to each letter, offering a different excuse for late payment in each case.

UNIT 21

Applying for a position

Helen has decided to leave National Plastics Ltd. She has gained experience in every department, and now feels that she would like to work for a smaller firm in which she could hold a more senior position. Accordingly she is replying to an advertisement in the Daily Gazette. The Managing Director of Anglo-Asian Agencies Ltd. requires an executive secretary who has the necessary experience to run the company for him when he is abroad on business trips. He is offering a very high salary. Helen wrote as follows:

A

```
                                               17 Wallace Drive,
                                               Finchley  Park,
   The Managing Director,                      London, NW3 H7D
   Anglo-Asian Agencies Ltd.,
   708 - 710 Commercial Towers,                1st February 198-
   New Oxford Street,
   London, W1X 2LR


   Dear Sir,

   With reference to your advertisement in today's edition of the Daily
   Gazette for an executive secretary, I shall be grateful if you will
   consider me for the position.

   I am 23 years of age and possess Fastsec Certificates in shorthand
   (100 words a minute) and typing (80 words a minute).  I have a working
   knowledge of commercial French and German.  I am at present studying
   Japanese.

   I attended the City Girls' High School in Finchley until I was sixteen
   and obtained my General Certificate of Education in six subjects,
   including Grade A in English, French, German and mathematics.  After
   leaving school I took the two-year secretarial course at the Fastsec
   Secretarial College and obtained their certificates.

   My first position was with Timly & Hunt & Co., chartered accountants,
   of 14 Chancery Lane.  I worked with them as a shorthand typist for
   one year.  I resigned in 1979 in order to take up a position as a
   junior secretary in the sales department of National Plastics Ltd.,
   where I am now working.  Since joining National Plastics I have worked
   in the sales, purchasing and accounts departments and have acquired
   I believe, a sound knowledge of day to day commercial practice.  I am
   now seeking employment with a firm in which I can assume wider respon-
   sibilities and, in time, obtain an executive, instead of a secretarial
   position.

   I can arrange to attend for an interview whenever convenient to you,
   but would appreciate 48 hours notice.  References concerning my character
   and ability can be obtained from Timly & Hunt & Co., and from
   National Plastics Ltd.

   I hope you will be able to give my application your favourable
   consideration.


   Yours faithfully,

   Helen Parsons

   Helen Parsons
```

The Managing Director of Anglo-Asian Agencies was impressed by Helen's letter. He was also impressed by a letter from another applicant, a Mr John Thornton. He asked his secretary, who was leaving to have a baby, to ask both to attend for an interview. He also asked his secretary to take up the two applicants' references. These were the letters she wrote:

B

Dear ...

Thank you for your letter applying for the position of executive secretary with this firm.

We shall be pleased if you will attend for interview on Wednesday 21st February at 3 p.m.

Will you please telephone me at 468756 and let me know whether or not you are free to attend for intervew at this time.

Yours sincerely,

Dawn Kemp

Dawn Kemp
Secretary to Mr Trevor Rumpus

To the companies given as references by the applicants, Dawn wrote as follows:

C

Dear ...

Mr/Ms ..., who has applied to this company for the position of executive secretary, has given us your name as a reference.

We shall be grateful for any information you can let us have about him/her. Such information will, of course, be treated in the strictest confidence.

Thank you for your assistance in this matter.

Yours faithfully,

Dawn Kemp

Dawn Kemp
Secretary to Mr Trevor Rumpus

Helen and John both informed Dawn that they could attend for interview at the time stated, and they were both duly interviewed by Mr Rumpus. He was impressed by both of them and decided to postpone making a decision until he received replies from their referees.

Helen's reference from National Plastics Ltd. was as follows:

D

Dear Sir,

With reference to your request for information about Miss Helen Parsons, we can tell you that she has worked for this company for two years, during which time she has worked as a secretary in our sales, purchasing and accounts departments.

We have found her to be thoroughly reliable and hard-working. Her pleasant personality has made it easy for her to make many friends here. She is an extremely efficient secretary, and we are sorry that she has decided to move on.

She has our warmest recommendation for any senior secretarial position.

Yours faithfully,

H. Wise

Herbert Wise
Personnel Manager

John Thornton's previous employer wrote:

E

Dear Sir,

Thank you for your letter of 16th February.

Mr John Thornton worked for this company as a clerical assistant from 1st September last to 31st January this year, when he resigned of his own accord.

We regret that we are unable to provide any further information about him.

Yours faithfully,

Judy White

Judy White,
Personnel Manager

Trevor Rumpus made his decision, and Dawn wrote on his behalf to the two applicants, as follows:

F

Dear Miss Parsons,

Thank you for attending for interview for the position of executive secretary. We are pleased to be able to offer you the position at a starting salary of £5,000 per annum.

You will receive four weeks annual holiday and, after a probationary period of three months, become eligible to join the company's super-annuation and health schemes, details of which are given in the enclosed leaflet.

We should like you to start work on Monday, 1st March at 9 a.m. Please let me know by return if you can accept this position.

Yours sincerely,

Dawn Kemp

Dawn Kemp
Secretary to Mr Trevor Rumpus

G

Dear Mr Thornton,

Thank you for attending for interview for the position of executive secretary to this company.

We have to inform you that the position has now been filled.

Yours sincerely,

Dawn Kemp

Dawn Kemp
Secretary to Mr Trevor Rumpus

Helen, of course, was delighted to be offered the job, and she replied by return, as follows:

H

Dear Sir,

Thank you for offering me the position of executive secretary. I am pleased to accept it.

I shall report for work on 1st March as requested.

Yours faithfully,

Helen Parsons

Helen Parsons

Helen then wrote a brief letter of resignation to National Plastics, as follows:

Dear Mr Wise,

I have been offered, and have accepted, the position of executive secretary with Anglo-Asian Agencies Ltd. I am writing, therefore, to give four weeks' notice, and wish to resign from the company on 28th February.

I trust that this will be convenient.

Yours sincerely,

Helen Parsons

Helen Parsons

I

Answer these questions about the letters in complete sentences.
1 What were Helen's qualifications?
2 What was her experience?
3 What references did she give?
4 Why did she apply for the position with Anglo-Asian Agencies?
5 When was she asked to attend for an interview?
6 What did she do on receipt of the letter from Anglo-Asian Agencies?
7 What did Anglo-Asian Agencies ask National Plastics Ltd. to provide?
8 Why did Trevor Rumpus postpone a decision as to which applicant he would employ?
9 Why do you think he did not give the job to John Thornton?
10 How did National Plastics Ltd. describe Helen?

11 What were the terms of Helen's appointment with Anglo-Asian Agencies?
12 Why did Helen write to National Plastics Ltd.?

Practice exercises

A
Study the third and fourth paragraphs of Helen's letter of application, and then write a paragraph for each of the following. Use the sentence patterns given below:
1 John—Borough Boys' School—17 years of age—one year secretarial course—first job: Pop Shop—junior clerk—6 months—City Discos—secretary—12 months
2 Alice—St. Eve's Convent—16—two year secretarial course—Star Insurance—typist—World Wide Travel—junior secretary—2 years

I attended ... until ...
After leaving school, I ...
My first position ... as a ...
I stayed for ...
I am now working with ... as ...
I have been working here for/since ...

B
People change their jobs for many different reasons, but the reasons given in letters of application are usually one or more of the following:

The applicant seeks a firm that provides/offers:
greater responsibilities
prospects for promotion
opportunities for advancement
further training
wider experience
a position in keeping with (my) qualifications and experience
greater job satisfaction
better pay

Complete the following statements with one of the reasons listed above. Make any necessary changes.
1 I am seeking employment in a firm which offers ...
2 I am seeking employment in a firm in which I can obtain/expect ...
3 I am seeking new employment in order to ...
4 I am seeking employment in a firm where there will be ...
5 I am looking for an opportunity to obtain/acquire ...

C
References
A former employer rarely makes critical comments about an unsatisfactory employee. He prefers to say nothing (see the letter concerning John Thornton). When an employee has given good

service, however, a good employer will usually do what he/she can to help him/her get a better job. The following are the key expressions:

rely on/reliable/reliability

depend on/dependable/dependability

can be trusted/trustworthy/trustworthiness

a hard worker/hard working (also *conscientious,* but do not use *diligent*)

efficient/efficiency

Express each of the following in a different way.
Example: Helen Parsons worked efficiently.

           (a) We found Helen Parsons to be efficient.

           (b) We were impressed by her efficiency.

1 We could rely on her.
   We found . . .
2 She was dependable.
   We could . . .
3 She could be trusted.
   We were impressed by . . .
4 She worked hard.
   We found . . .

D

Write a letter of application for the position of confidential secretary (or another position you would prefer) at the City & National Bank, mentioning whatever qualifications and experience you think are appropriate for the position. Give your reason for applying for the position and two references.

E

Now imagine that you are one of the employers given as references in your letter of application above. Write a letter of reference for yourself.

Glossary

Each word or expression is listed once only, for the unit in which it first appears, and with the meaning that applies in this context. However, if a word is used later with a different meaning, it is listed again. The words are given in alphabetical order for each unit, and may appear in the dialogue, the letters and/or the exercises.

UNIT ONE

at your earliest convenience: as soon as you can

brochure: booklet (small, thin book, usually with a paper cover) giving details of service (tours) offered

by return of post: immediately; by the next post

catalogue: list of available goods, carefully arranged with items numbered for easy finding and ordering

charter flight: flight on a plane specially hired for the purpose; not a regular, scheduled flight

circular: printed advertisement or notice intended to be sent to many people for them to read

fare schedule: list of prices (for tours)

group tour rates: cost for a group of people booked together on the same tour

mail: post (used especially in American English, but now also used in British English)

prospectus: a printed statement explaining the advantages and services offered (by a business, etc.)

range: complete set of different models of the same kind of goods (here: models of pens)

UNIT TWO

Correspondence School: a school whose teachers and students exchange information and work by post

enclose: put something in an envelope (or package) with a letter

make a reservation: book a place (on the tour) in advance

sample: a small amount of a product, given away free

135

UNIT THREE

confirmation copy:	a typed copy (of the telegram) sent to the receiver after it has been dictated on the phone
filing cabinet:	a piece of office furniture with drawers in it for storing papers, documents, etc.
in the immediate future:	very soon; as soon as possible
make out (a ticket):	write out all the details (on a ticket)

UNIT FOUR

file (v):	put (papers or letters) into a file (a compartment of a filing cabinet)
forward (v):	send (usually by post)
meet your requirements:	satisfy you; do what you require
run out of (stock):	use up all the supply of something; have no more left (in stock)
stocks:	supplies
warehouse:	a building for storing large quantities of goods

UNIT FIVE

Accommodation Bureau:	an office which finds places (flats, rooms, etc.) for people to live in
connect (her to Mr W's room):	join (two people) by telephone
duplicate copy:	exact copy
deposit:	a part payment of money, made in advance so that the seller will not sell the goods to anyone else
executives:	people concerned with making and carrying out decisions, especially in business
fully booked:	full; completely sold out
in great demand:	very popular
in short supply:	scarce; difficult to obtain
make an early booking:	reserve a place some time before the required date
reservation card:	a printed card requesting a public lending library to keep a book for you so that you can be the next borrower
showroom:	a room where examples of goods for sale may be seen
submit an application:	make a written request for a loan, job, etc.
there is a heavy demand for:	many people want (it)

UNIT SIX

acknowledge receipt (of a letter):	write to say (a letter) has been received
bank draft:	a written order by one bank to another to pay a certain sum of money to someone

confirmation slip:	a small, usually printed, piece of paper sent to prove that a required action has been taken .
economy seats:	cheaper seats; seats in the economy class (not first class) of a plane
full payment:	payment of the total amount owed
in due course:	without too much delay
on behalf of:	in the name of; as a representative (of the club)
photocopying machine:	a machine that makes photographic copies of letters, documents, etc. (also: **photocopier**)
postal order:	a kind of cheque, bought from a post office and sent to someone by post. The receiver can exchange it for the stated amount of money at another post office
receipt (for payment):	a written statement that money has been received
register my name:	put my name on the list of people (attending a course)
subscription:	money paid in advance for goods to be received regularly over a fixed period (here: a year)

UNIT SEVEN

account (of a customer):	record or statement of money owed
accountant:	a person whose job is to keep and examine the records of money received and paid by a business
balance:	the remainder; the difference between what has already been paid and what is still owed
balance due:	money still owed
credit:	a system of buying goods or services when they are wanted and paying for them later
credit an account:	make an entry on the credit side of a customer's account, showing that he has paid this amount
deal with them on a cash basis:	do business with a customer by selling goods or services for immediate payment
debit an account:	make an entry on the debit side of a customer's account, showing that he owes this amount
despatch an order:	send off goods ordered to the customer
invoice:	a bill for goods received (or sold)
issue:	supply or provide
loan:	amount of money lent (to someone)
Mail Order Book Company:	a company that sends books by post to a customer who has chosen them at home from a list or catalogue
on receipt of the balance:	when the balance has been received

open an account:	start keeping a record of money owed and paid by a (regular) customer
outline details:	the main ideas or facts
part payment:	an amount of money paid which is less than the total amount owed
Personal Loan Scheme:	a plan for lending money to an individual person (not to a business)
settle the balance due:	pay what is owed
statement (of an account):	a list showing amounts of money paid, owing, etc.
supply the order:	provide, send the goods ordered
tighten up our credit control:	become firmer or be more severe with credit customers who do not pay on time

UNIT EIGHT

amend:	improve by correcting errors
billed:	put on the bill
confirm:	give written proof (that something has been done)
day off:	a free day; a holiday from work
discount:	reduction in price allowed by the seller
files:	collections of papers, each on one subject, stored in a filing cabinet
let him down:	disappoint him by failing to give good service
overcharge (n):	an excess amount of money charged for goods

UNIT NINE

clerical error:	a mistake made by office staff
credit note:	a note issued by a shop when overcharges have been made, allowing the customer to buy goods of the same value as the overcharges
one gross:	twelve dozen (144)
personal calls:	private telephone conversations (made on an office telephone)
rectify an error:	correct a mistake
revised statement:	a new, corrected statement (of an account)
the line is engaged:	the telephone line (the number dialled) is busy, i.e. someone is using it

UNIT ELEVEN

credit account:	an account with a shop or company which allows the customer to take goods at once and pay later
delivery date:	the date on which goods will be handed over to the customer
import licence:	an official paper showing that permission has been given to import goods into a country

(not) a good credit risk: a company that can(not) be relied on to pay its debts

produce goods to our design: make goods exactly in accordance with the drawings or pattern that we will provide

representative: a person whose job is to sell a company's goods to other businesses, shops, etc.

stand (at an exhibition): a stall or small shop for showing goods

supply our requirements: provide the goods we need

terms of payment: conditions for paying for the goods

together with: as well as; in addition to

UNIT TWELVE

banker's draft: a **bank draft** (see Unit Six). A foreign exporter receiving a banker's draft may cash it at the local branch of the bank

against documents: on receipt of documents. The documents of 'Title to Goods' (ownership of the goods) are handed over only when the importer signs a 'bill of exchange'. This bill will state either that the importer has to pay immediately or that he must pay at a fixed future date

credit terms: conditions for opening a credit account

do overtime: work longer hours than usual

f.o.b.: (abbreviation for) **free on board:** the price includes delivery of the goods to the docks and putting them onto the ship

initial order: first order

instalment terms: conditions for paying by making small payments at regular intervals until the whole amount is paid

letter of credit: when a buyer from abroad agrees to pay by this method, he makes an arrangement with his bank. The bank instructs a bank in the UK to pay the exporter as soon as certain documents have been received and the exporter has fulfilled certain agreed conditions. If the L/C is **irrevocable**, it cannot be cancelled or changed except by agreement of all concerned

mailing list: a list of names and addresses kept by an organisation so that it can send regular information to these people by post

minimum order: the smallest quantity that can be ordered

monthly terms: conditions for paying by monthly instalments (see **instalment terms** above)

payment in advance:	payment made before the goods are received
quality plastic:	plastic of good quality
reference(s):	written information about a company's reliability in trade or (from a bank) confirming that the company has enough money in the bank to pay for the goods
under separate cover:	in a different envelope

UNIT THIRTEEN

Accounts	(the people working in) the accounts department of a company
attend to the formalities:	do everything necessary (in order to obey the rules and regulations of foreign trading)
backlog of orders:	orders that should have been dealt with before, but were not done at the proper time
cable:	a telegraphed message (it is sent by **cable:** a set of wires put underground or under the sea)
carbon:	(carbon paper) thin sheet(s) of paper, coloured on one side and used between sheets of writing paper for making copies
checked them out:	made all the necessary inquiries about them
despatch within 60 days:	send off in not more than 60 days
Further to:	in order to give additional information on the same subject (as in the previous discussion). This is a formal expression used mainly in business letters
Invoicing:	the department or office in which invoices (bills) are made out
Production:	the department (of a manufacturing company) which controls the producing of goods
proforma invoice:	an invoice which tells the customer the value of goods before they are despatched. It is not necessarily a demand for money, but usually requires confirmation by the customer
ream:	a measure for sheets of paper—480 sheets (UK) or 500 sheets (USA); 20 reams: 9600 or 10,000.
routine orders:	orders that are not unusual in any way
specifications:	details; detailed plan or set of descriptions
subject to:	on condition that; depending on
trial order:	a (usually small) order placed for the purpose of testing the quality of the goods before ordering a larger quantity

UNIT FOURTEEN

air freight: the transport of goods by air

cash on delivery (c.o.d.):   payment to be made when the goods are received

c.i.f.:   (abbreviation for) **Cost, Insurance and Freight;** all these are included in the price quoted

credit standing: the degree of business responsibility, reliability that a company is thought to have, especially with regard to paying debts

extend credit facilities to us: give us credit terms

gesture of good faith: an action done to show trust (in the company)

insurance: agreement by contract to pay money in case of accident, damage, etc.

investment: making more money by putting some money into something that will increase its value

occasional orders: not regular orders; orders placed from time to time

outstanding: not yet paid

pay in full: pay the whole amount

render an account: send an account of money that is owed

references: the people (or company or bank) that write references (see Unit Twelve) are also called **references**

restrict credit terms to…:   give credit only to…(not to anyone else) or, to give credit only for an agreed period of time

to date: up to the present time; until now

treated in the strictest confidence: considered as private and secret

well established: in existence for some time

UNIT FIFTEEN

before the due date: earlier than the agreed date

circumstances beyond our control: conditions or events which we have no power to control

covering letter: a letter containing additional information and sent with an invoice (or document, parcel, etc.)

invoicing clerk: the member of staff who makes out invoices

orders have to be invoiced: an invoice has to be made out for each order

resume supplies: begin to supply goods again after a period of not supplying them

see to them: deal with them; make sure they are done

subject to availability of stock: on condition that supplies of the goods are obtainable

UNIT SIXTEEN

carriage forward: transport to be paid by the receiver

discrepancies: errors; differences (between items, amounts, etc.)

overdue:	left unpaid too long
put on the market:	offered for sale to the public
take on temporaries:	employ **temporary staff**: staff who will have the job only for a limited period of time (the opposite of **permanent staff**)
take the matter up (with...):	discuss the subject (with...)

UNIT SEVENTEEN

a matter of urgency:	something that must be dealt with at once
casual workers:	workers employed without a contract of employment
foreign exchange rate:	the value of the money of one country compared with that of another
in this instance:	in this case; on this particular occasion
oversight:	unintentional failure to notice or do something
put it in hand:	begin to act; start negotiations
rough draft:	the first written form (of a letter); not in the finished, corrected form
take delivery:	receive (the goods)
to the letter:	exactly
under-staffed:	short of staff; (has) not enough staff

UNIT EIGHTEEN

authorising us to act on your behalf:	giving us power to act in your name
B/L, Bs/L,	(abbreviations for) **Bill(s) of Lading**: document(s) used in foreign trade, which serve as proof that the goods have been taken on board the vessel and without which the customer cannot clear Customs (see below)
buy in bulk:	buy (goods) in large quantities
Cat. No.:	abbreviation for **Catalogue Number**
clear Customs:	to get goods through Customs having satisfied Customs regulations (see **Customs** below)
collate:	collect and arrange in order
Commercial Invoice:	invoice. The term 'commercial' distinguishes it from other kinds of special invoices (not dealt with in this book)
components:	any of the parts that are needed to make up a whole (product)
consignment:	a number of goods sent together to a person or place for sale
Country of Origin:	the country where the goods came from
Customs:	the government organisation which collects taxes on goods entering the country

142

economy of scale:	buying things more cheaply because the larger the quantity of goods bought, the cheaper they are
effect Customs clearance:	clear Customs (see above)
endorsed:	signed
H.M. Customs and Excise:	(**H.M.**: Her Majesty's) the full title of the government organisation which collects tax on goods entering the country (**Customs**) and on certain goods manufactured and used in the UK (**Excise**)
indent (v & n):	(to make) a written order for goods to be purchased or supplied
in triplicate:	3 copies, the top copy being the original
inventory:	a list of all the goods, items in a place
minimise costs:	to reduce costs to the lowest possible amount
M.V.:	Merchant Vessel (for ships used for trade)
prevailing:	existing at the present time
processing:	going through a set of routine actions in examining, and checking (the requests)
raw materials:	the natural substances from which an article is made
sea freight:	transport of goods by sea, ship
standardise:	make all alike
transfer (from ... to ...):	move (from one place to another)

UNIT NINETEEN

as per:	according to
cover the deficiency:	make up for (in money) the amount that is missing (in goods)
deficiency:	something missing
forthwith:	immediately
misprint:	a mistake in printing
refund:	repayment; return of money paid
sight draft:	a bill of exchange, or an order in writing from one person to another, or to a bank, to pay on demand (at sight) a certain sum of money to the person named in the bill

UNIT TWENTY

A1 credit rating:	very good **credit standing** (see Unit Fourteen). (Credit) **rating** is used more in American English and (credit) **standing** is more usual in British English
adverse trading conditions:	conditions that are unfavourable (not good) for carrying on business
audited:	examined officially by a **chartered accountant** (see Unit Twenty-One below)

container ship:	a trading ship that carries very large metal boxes (containers) in which goods are packed
current:	present; of the present time
economic recession:	a period of reduced activity in industry, trading, etc.
lapsed:	came to an end
reasonable grounds:	acceptable, sensible reason
reminder:	a letter to make (them) remember
strongly worded:	firm; expressed very firmly, severely
submitted:	sent
overlooked:	failed to notice

UNIT TWENTY-ONE

chartered accountant:	an accountant who has passed all the official examinations and has full professional recognition
confidential secretary:	a secretary trusted with private matters
day to day commercial practice:	routine work of a commercial organisation
duly interviewed:	interviewed as and at the time expected
eligible to join:	able to join; suitable for joining
executive secretary:	a secretary with powers to make and carry out decisions
in keeping with:	suitable for
job satisfaction:	pleasure and contentment in one's work
leaflet:	a small, often folded sheet of printed matter, usually given free to the public
of his own accord:	without being asked
probationary period:	a fixed period of time for testing a person's character, ability, etc. in order to decide whether he or she is suitable for a position or job
prospects for promotion:	reasonable hope and expectation of getting a higher position at one's work
references:	written information concerning a person's character, ability and suitability for a job (compare **references** in Unit Twelve)
superannuation scheme:	a plan for providing people with a pension (money) when they retire from work in old age

Index of Functions and Structures

Any one business letter normally needs to do more than is indicated by a single 'letter-type' heading, for example a 'letter of apology' is likely to contain (a) a reference to a previous letter of complaint (b) an apology (c) an explanation and (d) a description of any action to be taken to correct the error that made the apology necessary.

This index identifies various communication areas and the student can refer to these to pick out suitable examples of language to use in a particular letter.

The examples in the index are usually taken from the practice exercises of the book; numbers refer to the unit in which a structure is practised. The letters D and L show that the structure is practised in the exercises that follow either the Dialogue (D) or the Letters (L); if neither letter appears, the structure is used in both parts of the unit. Occasionally, an asterisk (*) shows that the structure appears only in the Dialogue or Letters (not in the exercises), but is considered sufficiently useful to include in the index.

In general, examples from the Dialogues contain less formal language than that from the Letters. Where a 'D' example is also formal, this is noted (fml). Also, where an expression or structure is extremely formal (even in a business letter), this is also marked (fml).

The vocabulary in the examples may, of course, be adapted to suit any required situation.

145

INDEX

DESCRIBING ACTIONS

148

OPINION

giving an o.	I think we should be careful about...	15D
	I don't think we should do it.	15D
	(fml) we consider it would be (in)appropriate for you to...	14L
asking for an o.	we should be grateful if you would let us know whether, in your opinion, the amount...is appropriate	14L*

PAYMENT

sending p. by post	our deposit of £50 } our cheque for £2000 } is enclosed full payment of £465 }	6L
	I enclose a bank draft for £25	6L
describing method of p.	they enclosed a deposit of £50 with their letter	6D
	payment must be made in advance by irrevocable letter of credit	12L
	we shall pay for the goods by banker's draft	13L
asking about a preferred method of p.	Which would you prefer? To pay cash or to pay monthly?	14D
	Which will/would be more convenient for you? To pay cash or to...?	14D
stating preference	I'd prefer to pay cash/monthly	14D
	it will/would be more convenient for me/them to pay cash	14D
considering method of p.	are we prepared to... supply B.S. on credit?	13D
	accept payment by banker's draft?	13D
discussing late p.	their account should have been paid two months ago	20D
	it was due (to be paid) two months ago	20D
	it is now two months overdue	20D
demanding p.	we must insist on (immediate) payment of your account	20D
discussing accounts	we have received a deposit of £50	7D
	the balance due to us is £560	7D
	we debited their account with £798	7D
	we credited their account with £300	7D
	this left a balance due to us of £498	7D
	How much did they still owe W.W.T.? They still owed £798	7D